# SAARC

## Goals and Achievements

# SAARC

## Goals and Achievements

**Dr. Shailja Asthana**

M.A. (Political Science), Ph.D

Head, Deptt. of Political Science

Veer Bahadur Singh Govt. Degree College

Campeirganj, Gorakhpur

**Goel Publications**

**New Delhi - 110002**

**SAARC: Goals and Achievements**



First Published in 2021

ISBN 978-81-944886-7-1

₹ 795



*Published by* : **Goel Publications**
G-Floor, 4855/24, Ansari Road,
Daryaganj, New Delhi - 110002
Tel. : 9999819813
E-Mail: goelpublications@gmail.com

*Laser Typesetting* : Aarati Computers, Delhi-110 009

*Printed at* : Balaji Offset, Delhi

# Contents

# Preface

South Asia has long been recognized as distinct in the world, marked out by geographical contiguity, but also by the socio-economic and cultural commonalities. It has been quite late in walking up to the need for regional co-operation till 1985. South Asia was the only region in the world that had no own regional organization. The SAARC was established in 1985 in Dhaka, the capital of Bangladesh. The main objectives of SAARC are to promote the welfare of the people of South Asia, accelerate economic growth and increase collaboration and mutual assistance in economic, social, cultural, technology and scientific fields.

The present work is to focus on the divergence situation of South Asia and trace out the possible areas of co-operation. This is an in-depth study of SAARC. The work is based on the review of books relevant periodicals, newspapers, official speeches and documents. The historical, analytical methodology has been used to make this study non-dogmatic in focus, well balanced in coverage and interdisciplinary in approach. This book deals with the theoretical aspect and importance of regional organizations, as well as the concept of region and regionalism. In this work discussed of Aims and objectives of SAARC and find out the possible areas of co-operation. Further it also explained the structure and functions of SAARC including different SAARC Summits, conclusions and observations have been made.

*— Dr. Shailja Asthana*

# Acknowledgment

With the Blessings of God and 'Ashirvaad' of my parents I am fortunate to have complete this work. In the accomplishment of this book, many peoples have encouraged and helped me.

First of all, I express my regards to Prof. S.K. Jha, Ex. HOD of Political Science, D.D.U. Gorakhpur University, Gorakhpur. I want to express my gratitude to Hon'ble Prof. Shriprakash Mani Tripathi, Vice Chancellor of Indira Gandhi National Tribal University, Amarkantak and Mrs. Sheela Tripathi for their continuous encouragement and guidance.

I need not hesitate to admit my deep sense of gratitude for continual, able and expert guidance and painstaking efforts of my most esteemed brother Dr. D.K. Asthana Ex. Principal, A.P.N. P.G. College Basti and Mr. P.K. Asthana Ex. Director, Ministry of Defence, New Delhi, sisters, sister-in-laws and kids of my family, specially Divyansh, Disha and Deeksha for their support. I express my heartiest gratitude to Mr. Manoj Shrivastav for inspiring me time-to-time about the completion of the book and Dr. Vijay Pratap Singh, Principal K.N.I.T., Sultanpur for active support.

I am thankful to entire teaching and non-teaching staff of V.B.S. Govt. Degree College, Campierganj, Gorakhpur.

Raj Publications, New Delhi also deserves my heartiest thanks. I am highly obliged to all those scholars and writers, whose work was very useful for me.

*— Dr. Shailja Asthana*

# 1

# Introduction

Regionalism has been a marked feature of International Relation of the present day world. Regional organisations, of varied nature and scope, have proliferated after the second world war, whilst regional doctrine attempted to describe and explain regionalism, assess its present promises and project its future prospects.

Regional co-operation is a 'characteristic' phenomenon of the post war period. As regards the developing countries, the concept of regional co-operation is referred to in the context of their quest for the establishment of a unified community for the purpose of economic development; furthermore, the failure to implement the programme of action of New Internationl Economic Order (NIEO) has led to increasing emphasis on the regional and inter-regional co-operation among the developing countries[1].

Regionalism as a phenomenon in International politics has been subjected to theoretical understanding and security since the beginning of the 1960s. Out of such attempts emerged that is known as the Regional Integration Theory, which was said to be converted with .... explaining how and why states cease to be wholly sovereign, how and why they voluntarily mingle, merge and mix with their neighbours so as to lose the factual attributes of sovereignty while acquiring new techniques for resolving conflicts between themselves. Regional co-operation, organizations, systems and sub-systems may help describe steps along the way but they should not be confused with the resulting definitions[2].

The underlying assumption of the theorists approach tends to be that the states in a given region would and should eventually attain political unification. A number of variables were identified. Formulated and explained to chart out the process and predict the patterns of the said unification. Such variables included 'background conditions' (like the size of units i.e., states, rate of transactions among them, pluralism, elite complimentarily and perception of dependence); 'Conditions at the time of Union' (like the governmental purpose, external pressures and powers of the Union) and 'process conditions' (like the decision making styles, rate of transaction in the union, adaptability of governments and external pressures)[3]. However, neither these identified variables helped in the proper understanding of the phenomenon of regionalism nor the predictions made on the basis of the analysis of these variables and underlying assumptions could be upheld and supported by the real world situation[4]. The result was that by the mid-seventies, one of the pioneer and strongest exponents of the Regional Integration Theory[5], Has confessed its 'shortcomings'.

The functionalist thrust in the Regional Integration Theory concerned itself mainly with economic and social aspects of regional co-operation activities. Simple defined, issues at lower it mean that Regionalism was collective actions at regional level to secure national goals[6]. In the functionalist thrust, unification and the loss of attributes of sovereignty was ignored. Instead, the main imphasis lay on reducing or side-tracking political aspects by initiating regional action on appropriate and possible level of decision-making authority[7]. The resulting complex web of productive and mutually advantageous interrelationships, which were likely to have different patterns and contents in different situations, could bind the regional state actors into a system of interdependence. Such interdependence was expected to keep political and strategic conflicts sub-dued in the region by creating such social and economical relationships of profit and advantage that would involve heavy costs if allowed to break or weaken[8].

The existing theoretical approaches to Regionalism when applied to specific third world regions and situations will prove to be, if not totally irrelevant and misleading, at best inadequate. This is due to various factors, the most important of which is that there are vital differences between the situations obtaining at present in the third world regions and those in the West, particularly Europe, when steps towards Regionalism were initiated and advanced there. The existing Regionalism theory suffers from a European cultural bias as Western Europe has been the main focus and concern in its formulation. Even while studying the third world regions within the framework of this theory, the underlying assumption seems to have been maintained that the European experience or experiment in Regionalism will be followed and replicated[9].

The Integration theory including its functionlist thrust, reflects its main preoccupation with the socio-economic interests and pressure groups as the main agents of regionalism. These agents being well developed and powerful have been effective in Europe where, to some extent, they even succeeded in putting selective constraints on the Nation-State as a principal political actor. As a result, the socio-economic forces, in some limit but significant ways, could transact through the political barriers of sovereignty, nationalism, governmental priorities and bureaucratic procedures. This was possible because the socio-economic productive forces in Europe had reached a certain level of development so as to be able to exercise decisive influence. The productive forces of Europe also enjoyed considerable national and regional autonomy because the continent was not under colonial rule like the third world, and it dominated the world scene through its extended empires rather than being controlled by the external forces. In addition to this, political disharmonies and dissensions in Europe had been sorted out in a series of European conflicts that eventually culminated in the first and the second world wars[10].

When the International system was crafted after World War II. The Third World was still in the bloated wombs of the colonial empires of the imperialist powers of Europe, only stirring to be born into sovereign nations. The architects of the UN had global visions, the design that emerged under the gathering shadows of the cold war was also global. The only struggle that occurred between Regionalism and Globalism was between the United States and its Latin American neighbours.

The institutional approach to Regionalism and Regional co-operation that was incorporated. in the UN charter, founded on the clashing power politics of the two power blocs in the post-war years. The disfunctioning of the UN framed International system generated a new Western approach to world politics. It is known as the world order approach.

This approach has been developed at the theoretical level. Its fundamental premise is that the present structure of the International system is incapable of coping with the problems that beset it. These problems, which are global in nature are the growing arms-race, population explosion, decline of natural resources while demand for them grows; and growing danger to the ecology of the planet. Being global dangers, their mitigation lies in taking concerted action which would transcent national boundaries. However, a major problem emerges here. The fundamental actor in the International system is the nation-state. This unit is, by its very nature, self-seeking and inward-looking and therefore, cannot co-operate with other self-same units to check the dangers which threaten its existence. World order model builders therefore, believe that it is necessary to change the existing structure for it prevents the co-operation needed to check the dangers which threaten humankind.

Regionalism is seen as developing supranational attitudes thereby lefting both the individual and the nation-state from domestic loyalties. It is also viewed as a necessary agent to preserve the diversities of the International system. Regional Organisations are useful because while fostering diversity, they help to built the supranational attitude which is to be used as a stepping stone for allegiance to a global mechanism[11].

World order models have not been experimented with. Nor is there any reliable evidence that outlines of New Regional Orders and a New Global Order are emerging. Richard Folk, the best known protagonist of the world order approach, argues that the growing concern about nuclear proliferation might see the emergence of concerted action through the UN to prevent the drift[12]. This has not happend. Supplier countries have preferred to rely on unilateral measures like the Glenn-Symington Amendment or group action like the so-called London club. The proliferation drift has not been arrested. Besides, the world order approach does not command credibility in the Third world. only a handful of Third World scholars have paid serious attention to it[13].

The emergence of Regionalism was first seen in the Western Hemisphere and in Western Europe. The United Nations Charter also makes provisions for regional arrangements. Therefore, this concept is not contrary to the UN charter as it is misconceived by some people. The trend of Regionalism is in part an outcome of the necessity of pooling national resources for protection in a divided and war threatend world, but it is also an outgrowth of other pressures which are driving nations together in the present era. In recent years the pattern of International Relations is dominated by the Nation-State system for quite sometime. In this system, the regional groupings of states will be more important in comparison to modern independent sovereign nations. As Walter Lippmans says, "the true constituent member of the international order of the future are communities of states".

The concept of regional organizations was provided by the political-economic challenges thrown by the war and the states have been required to respond to them to protect and enhance their national interests. Chapter 8 of the UN charter recognises the rights of states to form regional organizations though the reference has been directly to the maintenance of International peace and security. There seems to be no reason not to inject a liberal interpretation and extend the scope of regional organizations to other fields as well as particularly when the term 'peace' has been widely interpreted to have included the idea of economic development[14].

## Concept of Region

Before discussing Regionalism, it is better to define the term 'Region'. The words 'Region' and 'Regional Organizations' have given rise to much confusion and difficulty in their application to Inter-Governmental Organizations. The term 'Region' in abstract is politically meaningless. One might ask in relation to what subject matter is the term used in any particular context ? It is clear that what is a region for one purpose may not be region for another. Geographically, Europe has, for example, proved in practice to be a region for many purposes of technical character, such as transport or environmental. But Geographically Europe has not yet proved to be Region for most economic or political purpose. Then there are so called Functional/Regional Organizations, such as the Organization for economic co-operation (OECD), whose membership cuts across geographical continents. To avoid all this confusion, therefore, a region is treated as a convenient geographical continents are controlled by sovereign governments, whose interest in any particular subject is sufficiently compatible for them to be able to enter into effective multilateral co-operation.

The notion of a 'Region' either within a single country or a region of the world embracing a number of nations has provided a venerable tool in the workshed of political and social research. A region is a unit on the basis of which the study is done. As far as meaning of 'Region' is concerned, normally it means smaller than states but the understanding of the term in the context of International Relations has two cannotation. Firstly a region is invariably an area, embracing the territories of three or more states. These states are bound together by ties of common interests as well as of geography. Secondly, those areas where 'far-flung' and geographically scattered nations from an association, or 'a real community of states for common interests. The outstanding example of for flung Regionalism is the association of fifteen nations, on both besides of the Atlantic and in the Scandinavian and Mediterranean areas, in the North Atlantic Treaty.

In fact, a region has been defined by Bruce M. Russet as an ordinary, common and practical geographical area 'for which social and economic improvement programmes have been conceived, planned and undertaken'[15].

A region is more than a country but less than a continent. It may be regarded as a geographical area having at least three states within it which are objectively recognised as constituting a distinctive community, region or segment of the global system. 'Regional co-operation implies association among such states 'to promote common goals, meet common needs and resolve common problems'. The commonality of interest is..... the central motivating force for their co-operation on a regional basis and also for determining the modality, including institutional arrangements for such co-operation[16].

The idea of regional co-operation has acquired a new momentum in the context of the changed world economic situation. The lack of enthusiasm among the developed countries of the North in creating a New International

Economic order based on justice and equity and, on the contrary, their protectionism have provided an added urgency to the countries of the South for greater co-operation among themselves. Increasing generation of impulses among themselves and their transmission to other developing countries have now been regarded to be essential for the attainment and sustenance of a relatively high tempo of growth. The resultant self-reliance would enhance the bargaining power of the South with the North. South-South co-operation, therefore, instead to being left to chance, must be pursued conciously and South-South linkages built up deliberately through the creation of systems and mechanisms among the developing countries both at the global and at the regional levels[17].

It soon becomes obvious that different criteria for identifying regions yield together different regional configuration. The following criteria are commonly use for regions :

(a) Geographical Criteria of Region : It means the geographical location of the member countries in continents, subcontinent archipelagoes etc. for instance Europe and Asia.

(b) Economic Criteria of region - It means grouping nation-states on the basis of selected criteria of economic development, such as gross national product and industrial output, e.g. industrialised versus transitional versus less developed states.

(c) Military and Political Criteria - It means the grouping of a Nation-State on the basis of their participation in alliance or on the basis of ideological and political orientation, e.g. NATO, WARSAW pact, communist Bloc etc.

(d) Transnational Criteria - The grouping Nation-States on the basis of volume and frequency of exchange of people, goods and services, such as immigrants, tourists, trade and messages, e.g. United States and Canada, the Western European Market area, the East

European - Soviet Market.

(e) The Collective Security Criteria- This criteria is the most fundamental and important criteria of region. Security of nations is the center point in that criteria.

On the basis of above mentioned criteria, a regional arrangement of states is made.

## Concept of Regionalism

Regionalism is a post world war phenomenon and this concept is sometimes put forward as an alternative to Globalism, a superior substitute for the principle of University. Further, Regionalism has been a product of world politics, initiated mostly by great powers in the regions adjacent to them or even far off, to seek a desirable regional order for a global balance that could cater to their respective regional and group interests[18]. However, Regionalism in a functional term denotes a preferential approach to problem-solving based on factors common to a region, or to a group, or to the policies advanced on the particular subject matter[19].

The roots of Regionalism can be found in the cultural foundations of common loyalities, the objective similarity of national problems, and the potential awareness of common interests which are necessary for the effective functioning of multilateral institutions[20]. The world is too diverse and unwiedly; the distances-physical, economic, political, security and cultural between peoples at opposite ends of the earth are too formidable to permit development of working sense of common involvement and joint responsiblity. Moreover, regional approaches, offer a framework for negotiation or functional co-operation. The famous American Scholar Joseph S. Nye argues that Regionalism or Regional Organization is the next big step forward in International co-operation and "an important middle ground" between the individual nation and a federation of the world[21].

Nevertheless, regional organizations have grown rapidly

in the post quarter century and regionalist doctrines have likewise increased. Scholars have reffered to Regionlism as "the dominant note of the contemporary world"[22]. However, Regional Organizations are very limited in scope but some are broader in ambitions. Academic Authors have also used the term "Regional Organizations" in a variety of ways. Some use the term "Regional" for all organizations which are not global in their membership and these are selective organizations which restrict membership on the basis of geographical principle. These organizations are distinguished by their official or formal function like military, security, political, diplomacy and economic development. The scholars characterize the regional organization in the two types; "Micro Regional Economic Organizations" that are relevant to integration and "Macro Regional Political Organizations" that are involved in controlling conflict among their members. In addition the experts of International law have also used the term "Regional Organization" which restricts it membership, in principle and in practice, on the basis of geographical contiguity[23].

Several definitions, however, have been advanced by various scholars on the Regionalism; According to Thomas Frank: "A Regional Organization is any grouping of States in some defined geographical context with historic, ethnic or socio-political ties, which habitually acts in concert through permanent institution to foster unity in wide range of common concern[24].

Bruch M. Russett offers four criteria indication of Regionalis, namely, social and cultural homogeneity, shard political attitudes and behaviours, political interdependence and geographical proximity[25].

So, to Russett, any regional arrangement fulfilling the above criteria may aptly be considered as such. These criteria may not, however, be found in areas which are normally identifie as regions. West Asia, for example, is often identifie as a region, but the presence of Israel in the area prevents any congruence between the region as a whole and the phenomenon of Regionalism within it. Similarly, India and Pakistan are supposed to belong to the region of South Asia, but it one goes by Russett's criteria, Regionalism does not exist in the area.

The above difficulty has led some writers to view the concept of Regionalism in an elastic form. Alf. Ross, opines that the expression 'Region' does not require that the participating states in a regional arrangement shall be within a certain geographical proximity[26].

Ross expresses the view that in Article 53(1)[27] ofthe UN charter, the expression "Regional Arrangement" is used with reference to mutual assistance treaties concluded between states without any such connexion of regional propinquity of states forming such as arrangements. Norman Benturch and Andrew Martin argues on similar lines-that although, ordinarily a 'Region' may mean a limited geographical area, yet at San Francisco, a proposal made for the inclusion, in the text of the UN Charter of a strict definition, based primarily on geographical proximity of 'Regional Arrangement' was rejected, thus undercutting the geographical propinquity contention[28].

Some scholars have distinguished between a "Regional System". A regional organization in Joseph Nye's view, is based on a formal agrument among governments, possessing diplomatic forums and assisted by a associated International bureucracy. Accordingly, Nye opines that the concept of 'regional system', which he defines as "a regular pattern of International among independent political units in a region", is broader than the term "Regional Organization"[29].

Thus firstly, Regionalism in its broadest sense is a regional system, a regular pattern of interaction among political units, geographically proximate to each other. Secondly, Regionalism signifies the presence of the more particularistic regional organization, which is not necessarily congruent with the regional system. For example, the Arab League represents not the broader aspects of Regionalism (i.e., a regional system), but its more specific particularistic aspect (i.e., a regional organization). Thus Israel and the Arab states in their inter-state and intra-regional interactions, represent one aspect of Regionalism in West Asia and the Arab League, another aspect of Regionalism in the same area.

Besides, these essential differences between regional arrangements, proper and military alliances. Van Kleffen offers three factors which distinguish between these two catagories of regional arrangements. Firstly, in alliances, as distinct from regional arrangements proper, the accent is on closely concerted policy and action at all times, other than on a narrowly circumcribed object. Secondly, alliances may be offensive, while the aim of regional arrangements. In other words the collective element plays a greater part in regional arrangements than in alliances[30]. In sum, therefore, "a regional arrangement in International Politics may be described as some form of voluntary agreement or organization established to further joint action of states comprising, or having an interest in some geographical area which is either generally organised as a region or delimited by agreement[31].

## Regional Organizations

On the basis of orientation and the field of activity regional organization may be classified into three categories:

(i) Regional Political Organizations - The Regional Political Organizations have arisen mainly as the expression of some kind of regional solidarity in the face of politics of the outside world. There are also primarily concerned with the settlement of intra-regional disputes through diplomatic process or through limited peace-keeping machinery to control the use of force within the region. Besides, they may or may not present a common military or diplomatic front against an outside actor or actors e.g. the Organization of American States (OAS); The League of Arab States; the Organization of African Unity

(OAU); the Council of Europe, etc. The regional political organizations are described by some writers as "Macro-Regional Organizations[32] and "Original"[33] regional organizations.

(ii) Regional Military Organizations : The Regional Military Organizations function primarily in the Military Security share and are composed of States bound together by multi-lateral defence treaties designed to present a common Military, or diplomatic, front against an outside actor or actors. They are primarily established to counter any external threat to its members e.g. are the North Atlantic Treaty Organization (NATO); Treaty Organization (WTO); The Treaty between the United States, Australia and Newzealand. These are also called regional alliance organizations by some writers[34].

(iii) Regional- Functional Organizations : The Regional Functional Organizations are the Welfare - Oriented Organization dealing with economic, social, cultural and other non-political and non-Military aspects of international co-operation. They regard the Military Security component as or partialy or entirely irrelevant to the purpose of the organization and concern themselves with the mutual desire to improve economic relations and to deal with other technical problems resulting from proximity and growing interdependence. Examples of such organizations are the European Economic Community (EEC); The European Coal and Steel Community (ECSC); The Nordic Council; The Organization for Economic Co-operation and Development (OECD); The European Free Trade Association (EFTA); Council for Mutual Economic Assistance (COMECON); The Latin American Free Trade Association (LAFTA); The Central American Common Market (CACM); The Economic Community of West African States (ECOWAS); The Colombo Plan and others.

The first two of the above categories may be called as

"Security Regionalism" and the third one may be characterized as "Functional Regionalism". It needs be noted, however, that a regional organization today deft such classification because of their Multi-functional and Multi-dimensional patterns. The Common-Wealth of Nations, for example, does not fall under any of the three classifications, though it is sometimes described as a regional organization.

## Importance of Regional Organization

The rapid growth of independent States and the function of regional groupings of organization has become a trend in the world politics since the post World War II. A growing awareness of interdependence among the independent states, an imagination of a nation that its own interests are combined with those of other nations in similar conditions, that there is a complementarity not only in the similarity, but also in the disparity and the recognition of an amenable explanation of sovereignty have simulated the process of regional co-operation. Regional co-operation is true, a multi-dimentional process. The national attitude, the regional objectivity and the International perspectives can note its multiple aspects. Success in regional co-operation is by and large guided by the nature of accord that is inducted in these multiple angles. This harmony is sustained by effective policy formulations at the state level, on the one hand, and by the removal of barriers that restrain the process of co-operation, on the other.

Regionalism has, thus, become a viable policy alternative among the developing countries not only in elaborating the basic principles of their collective economic diplomacy but as a means in enhancing their positions at the numerous neighbours for a New International Economic Order since the late sixties. The success of European Economic Community (EEC) in fostering economic integration and helping fast economic recovery and industrial resilience in Western Europe popularised regional approach to economic co-operation in third world. From the late sixties, the third world countries have attempted vigorously by to work out regional committees in different parts of the world. Since then, most developing countries (including India) thought that the poor nations of the South could not help to progress rapidly unless five conditions in International Relation were achieved :

(i) There should be large flow of aid to South;

(ii) commodities should enjoy better access to the markets of North;

(iii) manufactured exports from South should get special concessions in the North under generalised scheme of performances;

(iv) South co-operation should be promoted;

(v) The North should lower its trade barrier under GATT while the South should remain free to raise its own barriers[35].

However, dispite strong rationale for achieving these conditions, the basis of mutual co-operation and joint interaction in these line of directions have been quite substantially departing not only from one country to other but also from region to region on account of the divergence in their economic capacities as well as internal political and socio-economic diversity either in settling on increased share of resources among themselves or in bargaining multually profitable interest in area of trade policy, regulation of multinations, transfer of technology, migration, food policy and above all the sentiments of people with regard to economic and the nature of development paradigm[36].

The whole world is moving towards regional economic arrangements for an organizational framework as well as gradual economic integration since the post - World War II. Unfortunately, despite subsequent efforts of the various multi-lateral global negotiation for improving the existing international economic order and internal economic reforms, there has been a growing multiplicity of tensions and difficulties which do not appear to have provided adequate political stability or economic viability to the developing world either in stemining out growing trade conflicts, clamity of resources crunch, volatility in monetary and financial system, fluctuations in exchange rates, uncertainities of capital market or in relegating deteriorating terms of trade, unmanagable balance of payments crisis, accute debt problem and persisting inflation. Even the oil price shocks that are being thrust on the world economy since 1973 by the oil producing countries, though leading to significant distorations in the balance of economic power and stability in the world economy and resulting in global clamity of continuous resources crunch and the balance of payments problem could not be settled to a manageable level on the basis of international negotiations as yet.

Under this uncertain international economic environment many low and middle income countries are not only struggling with falling rates of saving, mounting debt burden and the consequent debt, trap but also continuously facing the horror of stagnation, deteriorating terms of trade, unemployment and rapidly falling standard of living. In the socialist countries, major market-oriented economic reforms are being introduced for their radical transformation since 1980s[37]. An openners in the rigid theoretical framework of traditional socialist systems thus, gathered considerable momentum not merely because the principle command - oriented underdeveloped countries have experienced generally luckwarm economic performance but the major centrally planned economies including Soviet Union and China have acknowledge strain in their economies attributable in a large part to their overly quantitative and rigid command system. A massive rejection and the collapse of the deep-rooted communist regimes created by Lanin and Stalin in the whole of Eastern Europe for more than four decades and in Soviet Union for more than six decades after the 'coup' of August 19th, 1991 is now not only witnessing an acknowledgement in favour of market driven welfare states but also reflecting multiple centres of power in place of bipolar world. The low income countries, on the other hand, did not enjoy high growth rates during the period of world booms[38]. During 1980, their growth rates declined even more the middle income countries like Asian countries and South American countries which did exceeding by well during 1960s have become the major victims of current turmoil experiencing very low growth rates accompanied by very high debt and debt service ratio. They are even unable a cushion stocks emanating from adjustment and structural policies geared to market-oriented reforms. While the rich developed market economies have witnessed a crisis in major stock markets and exchange of the world[39], there is acute confrontations among the questions regarding resource flow, raw material prices, access to markets and technology. They are searching new policies to tide over the crisis.

On the other hand, the over-exploitation of basis global natural resources as a resuslt of rapid pace of industrialization in the developed and developing countries and the warming up of the earth's climate owing to "Gulf War" alongwith highly susceptible effects of the process of soil erosion, soil infertility, flood and other ecological disasters have now taken truely international dimensions in regarded to the question relating to interesting and puzzling interaction between the reduction of poverty and protection of the environment. Both the issues have created the most serious and urgent common threat to both the developed and developing countries and have led to the relation for the imperatives of the new concept of sustainable development[40].

The concept of fast global wave for technological transformation, it is obvious that almost all countries of rich developed market economies would have to face continuous multiplicity of strains and difficulties in making distinction between those technologies which would be highly required by industry in the years to come to facilitate demand in the market and the anticipate theose technologies that will decline in future in significance. This process would not only enhance the pace of creative destruction in the forms of high unemployment, acute demand recession and keen competition in search of new technologies of 'compete each other in the international market but would, add more costs and less benefits and consequently lead to perpetual construction of markets and deteriorating terms of trade. The fast changing technological conditions which demand high sofistication of development and huge capital investment, the developing countries such as SAARC region will have to evolve new strategies for safeguarding their interest keeping in view the availability of capital, indigenous capabilities for relevant innovations and adaptation of technologies.

Until the mid-eighties the rich developed market economies were at least abade on the extremity for achieving industrial and agricultural development in the middle and low income countries and were ready and agreeable to offer some real assistance towards bringing about this glob. However, from the begining of 1980s, there has been a fundamental change in the attitude of rich market economies for providing adequate funds for development to middle and low income countries. Today, although the quantum of assistance has increased. It is still less than half of what it was in the beginning of 1980s[41]. It is thus, evident that the conditionality for the inflow of aid or credit either from G-7 Group of multi-lateral lending agencies would likely to argument growing resources crunch and scarity of funds in Eastern Europe, Asia and less developed countries[42] and would seriously affect appropriate distribution of world resources, their efficient utilisation and thereby generate a growing demand recession and slow expansion of markets in the different countries of the world.

These sea-changes towards regionalisation in the world power structure and the emergence of multiple centres of power in place of bi-polar world would have a far-reaching impact on the economy and the policy of the SAARC region and thereby throwing a varieties of new challenges in many directions over a wide range of activities.

The economic costs and benefits are those which increase or decrease the unit costs and prices of goods and services and macro-economic and sectoral output growth rates in countries which enter into varying forms of regional economic co-operation. The favourable changes in unit costs and prices and growth rates may come about from the realisation of potential economic benefits from; lower intra - regional transport and transaction costs; more favourable terms of trade; inter-country, inter-sectoral and inter industry/sectoral complementarities and comparative advantages, economies of scale in investment, production and distribution; and, more generally, from increased external and entra-regional trade creation, and form higher efficiencies due to increased intra-regional competition and institutional co-operation. These factors could directly change the unit costs and prices and growth rates within a set of sectors in which economic co-operation is effected; but they could also favourably or unfavourably effect these economic indicators in other forward or backward liked sectors within the region.

The Political economic costs and benefits of regional co-operation are these which affect the socio-economic welfare levels of the co-operating countries as well as of sub-groups and sub-regions within these countries. The changes in welfare levels can be conceptualised in terms of employment and income/asset levels, specially, and the quality of life, more generally. Apart from this regional co-operation would also effect the relative bargaining power of the region as a whole as well as of countries, sub-groups and sub-regions vis-a-vis each other, and vis-a-vis their counterparts outside the region.

Regional political co-operation and understanding could lead a costs and benefits of a political - strategic nature. These could be in terms of greater regional and national political consensus and legitimacy and stronger political will and administrative and people's support to effect mutually beneficial co-operation in all areas of bilateral and multilateral concerns. Political co-operation could, furthermore, result in increased negotiating strength of the region vis-a-vis the multilateral and international institutions, other regional groupings, and national governments, on economic and political matters. It could additionally, contribute to the strengthening of the capabilities of national governments and regional mechanism to help resolve sensitive sub-regional and regional issues. Such co-operation could also, in principle, promote the evolution of regional approaches to strategic, defence and national security concerns, with their attendent implications for economic resources and developmental costs and benefits.

Some of these would be transitional and structural in nature, while others would be of a long-term nature. The former would effect sub-groups and sub-regions which could have to adjust to the restructuring of regional investment, production and distribution patterns in a framework of economic co-operation. The transitional economic costs would be primarily in terms of unfavourable change in income/asset and employment levels for the effected sub-groups and sub-regions. The longer duration or more permanent costs could also be in terms of some dilution of national and sub-national autonomy in policy formation in a regional framework of co-operation, particularly in macro-economic and developmental areas[43].

## Need For Regional Co-operation in South Asia

The need for Regional co-operation among the low developed countries was felt after the Second World War. During this period, the tide of national liberation movement in Asian countries is historically very important. The newly independent states emerged in this period were India, Pakistan, Cylon, Burma, Indonesia. These countries felt the use of regional co-operation to overcome political tensions and socio-economic problems during the second half of this century.

However, the lack of leadership, internal economic reorganisation, internal disturbances among these newly developed states stood other way to develop working out problems and concentrate on regional co-operation.

The success of European Economic Community (EEC) in helping the economic recovery of the West, popularised the need for economic co-operation particularly to the low developed countries.

Some progress has been made in a limited way in this direction through the ASEAN and ADB. But these could not exploit the fruits of regional co-operation for different reasons. As a result, seven South Asian countries - India, Pakistan, Bangladesh, Srilanka, Nepal, Bhutan and Maldives have formed the South Asian Association for Regional co-operation (SAARC) to facilitate broder regional economic co-operation and reduce tensions in this area.

Regional co-operation among South Asian countries are useful for different reasons. The economic co-operation among the capitalist countries have made West Europe a strongest force in the world. The weakness of individual countries in the international market and caused South Asian countries to fall into the debt trap of the West. In the United Nations the voice of these countries would be honoured if they sound same words together. What is more, regional co-operation may release the political tensions in South Asia. Almost all the seven countries have the same history, religion, culture, language. Thus, the joined hands to explore the fruits of regional co-operation in South Asia though SAARC[44].

From the economic point of view it can be pointed out that the demand for export of South Asian Countries have declined due to the discriminating policies of the traditional buyer countries of Asia[45]. Again, due to oil price hike imports of South Asian countries have increased[46]. For these reasons the South Asian countries should try to solve the problem of balance of trade within this region through mutually advantageous export and import.

Today almost all the countries must accept the fact that they are part of the world economy. No country can escape its role in the system of inter-dependent trading nations. It is still a debatable point whether the degree of interdependence among nations is increasing or not. But it is a fact that the world trade has grown exceptionally fast in the post-war years. On the whole, the forces working for economic interdependence among nations seen irresistible.

It is fact that the rich nations are getting richer, while the poor nations are trying to stand upon their own legs. One possible way to accelerate economic growth of the developing countries is through regional co-operation. Enhancing intra-regional trade is an important instrument of this overall approach. The dynamic complementarities among the developing countries in resources, skills, technologies and market opportunities have opend new vistas of opportunities among themselves. Well conceived and property implemented programmes in that direction would help countries of the South to reduce their dependence on the North as well their vulnerability to external trends and pressures. South-South co-operation has acquired definitive form and content during the past decade in the action programmes adopted at the successive NAM summits and by group of 77 at the U.N. The declaration and the programme of action on the New International Economic Order (NIEO) adopted by the U.N. in 1974, the U.N. conference on technical co-operation in 1978 etc. are the stepping stones towards establishing a framework of economic co-operation among developing countries.

The South-South co-operation, especially South Asian Regional co-operation is a new platform which has provided a new horizen for regional co-operation in South Asia. Such forum as is evident from various deliberations of SAARC's meetings, has identified new areas of co-operation which will go a long way in strengthening the co-operation of these member nations[47].

The present move of regional co-operation in South Asia has all the necessary ingredients to emerge as an ideal and genuinely autonomous example of collective self-reliance within the framework of South-South co-operation. Whether it really will, would however depend upon a number of imponderables and unassessed imperatives.

For regional co-operation is not simply all economic aspirations and rationally designed state actions. It is an outcome of a number of complex and mutually incompatible political, strategic and diplomatic initiatives, responses and interests amongst the states and their managers in a given region. This is what it was when regionalism as one of the most important goals of state policies. It was pursued by India and its Nehru, in a wider Asian context during the late forties and early fifties. This is what it is also when the initiative taken by the Late President Zia-ur-Rahman of Bangladesh in May 1980 is being gradually carried forward by leaders of the Seven South Asian Countries viz.- India, Pakistan, Bangladesh, Srilanka, Bhutan and Maldives Islands[48].

## Regionalism : An Appraisal

Regional organizations in International Politics has become a trend, which with the passage of time has been acquiring new dimensions. However, in many cases the arrangements or so unwidely that they could be best described as global system of national states rather than regional systems still regional organisations are growing in a faster rate and regional systems have become the established norm of the day.

Importance of a regional organisations or the utility, size, impact efficiency of its are relative terms. The most common bond is usually economic or security consideration.

Regional membership of a state in an exclusive regional club of nations does not necessarily means imply political cohesiveness. On the contrary certain amount of functional co-operation is sought to achieve certain national goals co-ordination is accentuated in some priority areas of common interest to influence the political environment. In such a way so as to make it suitable to the member nations preference.

The establishment of the common market and the European Court in the advanced region of the Western Europe must not be viewed as the touch stone of regionalism because multinational, multicultural, multilingual continent -like countries of Soviet Union or India are still facing the problem of national integration where subnational under currents are very much in flow, even with the administrative and state policies - mechanism. Compared to these countries, Western European regionalism has not achieved much.

Interestingly when some cultural lingual and ethnic affinities transcend national boundaries, they provide a case for regionalism. Thus while a national like India, because of the existence of subnational group like Tamils, or Bengalis, religious communities like Hindus, Muslims find it difficult to go for a composite national integration, it is for the same reason easier for her to have common bonds with Srilanka and Bangladesh or Nepal and Pakistan.

Thus the trend towards international regionalism is now an acknowledged feature of the international scene. It has achieved a new meaning and a new significance while it has not in my real sense breached the barrier of the sovereign state system, it has provided the impetus and the machinery for much closer co-operation of the states on the regional level. But it has been argued in certain quarters that the formation of regional organization has greatly undermined the position of the United Nations and posses a serious threat to the existence of the international organizations. Carlos Ramulo of Philippines observed that the United Nations is dying because the states are taking more and more the great political issues outside the framework of the organisation. Similarly Edgar. S. Furniss holds that the United Nations has been placed in a position of inferiority, that now the likes between the regional arrangements and the world organisation exist at the practical pleasure of the former. He further suggests that there is a great need to rethink the concept of regionalism[49].

However the above view is not universally accepted and majority of the scholars hold it as erroneous. This eroneous view largely exists because of the assumption that the regional organizations are also concerned with all the problems which are the concern of the United Nations and operate at cross purposes with the world body. Naturally, regional arrangements cannot be regarded as contradictory to the world body, though by definition regional systems are limited in their scope and functions. Overall, regional arrangements maintain a harmonious relationship with the world body.

International regionalism by way of gradual progress when develop into a closely integrated framework with a touch of catering to universal interests it plays a beneficial role in international politics. But if it remains synonymous with military blocs and alliances it would, of course, play a destructive role in today's world polities which is marked by mistrust and tensions.

## References

1. Julius K. Nyerere, "South-South Co-operation" in Altaf Gauhar ed. Third World Strategy: Economic and Political Cohesion in the South; (London, Third World Foundation, 1983), p. 10.
2. Earnst B. Haas, "The study of Regional Integration", Reflections on the Joy and Auguish of Pro-theorizing", International Organization, Vol. 24, Autum 1970, p.610. (This was a special issue on Regional Integration). Also by Haas, The Uniting of Europe: Political, Economic and social Forces,

1950-1957, Stanford University Press, California, 2nd ed. 1968).

3. Mario Barrera and Ernst B.Haas, "The Operationalization of some variables Related to Regional Integration: A Research Note", International Organisation, Vol. 23, no. l, Winter 1969, pp. 150-60, Philippe C. Schmitter, "Three Neo-Functionalist Hypotheses about International Integration", ibid, pp. 161-6; also his "Further Notes on operationalizing some variables Related to Regional Integration", International Organization, Vol. 23, no. 2, Spring 1969, pp. 327-36. To this Mario Barrera replied in the next issue of the Journal, pp. 969-70.

4. For critical comments and other case studies, see Leon N. Lindenberg and Stuart A. Sheingold, Regional Integration; Theory and Research, Harward University Press, 1971.

5. Ernst B. Haas, the obsolescence of Regional Integration Theory, Institute of International Studies, University of California, Berkeley, 1975; also his "Turbulent Fields and the theory of Regional Integration", International Organization, Vol. 30, Spring 1976, no.2, pp. 173-212.

6. James N.-Shubert, "Towards a working Peace System in Asia: Organisational Growth and state participation in Asian Regionalism", International Organization, Vol. 32, no. 2, 1978, pp. 425-62; For a standard functionalist definition of the regional integration process, see, David Mitrany, A Working Peace System, London, Royal Institute of International Affairs, 1946.

7. Shubert, n. 5: Joseph S. Nye, Peace in Parts: Integration and conflict in Regional Organizations, Boston, Little Brown, 1971, Also his, International-Regionalism, Boston, Little Brown, 1968; Stanley Hoffman, "Discord in Community; The North Atlantic Area as Partial International System", International Organization, Vol.17, Summer 1963.

8. Richard Rosecrance and Arthur Stein, "Inter-dependence: Myth or Reality" ? World Politics, Vol. 26, October 1973; Rosecrance et al., "Whither Interdependence"? International

Organization, Vol. 3l, Summer 1977, p. 429, Robert O. Kechane and Joseph S. Nye Jr., Power and Interdependence, Boston, Little Brown, 1977; also see Henery R. Nav, "From Integration to dependence: Gains, Losses and Continuing Gaps" (A review article) International Organisation, Vol. 33, no. 1. Winter 1979, pp. 119-47.

9. For example, see Schubert, n. 5, James Lawlwer and Jarome Laulichit, "International Integration in Developing Regions", Peace: Research Review, Vol. 3, no. 5, 1970; Aaron Segal, "The Integration of Developing countries. Some thoughts on Africa and Central America", Journal of Common Market Studies, Vol. 2, June 1967, W. Andrew Axline, "Under-development, Dependence and Integration', The Politics of Regionalism in third world", International Organization, Winter 1977, Vol. 31, no. 1, pp. 83-105. Lym Mytelka, "Regional Integration in the Third World; Some Internal Factors", in International Dimension of Regional Integration in the Third World, University of Ottawa Press, 1975.

10. S.D. Muni & Anuradha Muni, Regional Co-operation in South Asia, National Publishing House, pp. 2-3.

11. Bhabani Sen Gupta, "Regional Co-operation and Development in South Asia", 'Regionalism in South Asia: Role and Behaviour, pp. 1-2.

12. Richard A. Falk, The Endangered Planet, New York, Random House, 1971, pp. 334-40.

13. In India, Rajni Kothari is a noted protagonist of the world order approach. The Centre for Study of Developing Societies co-sponsors Alternatives, a World Order Journal of which he and Folk are joint editors.

14. Bipattaran Ghosh, "SAARC; Some Major Impediments to its success", Asian Studies, Vol. XIII, no. 1, 1992, p. 30.

15. Bruce M. Russet, 'International Regions and International system', cited. in P.Ke Mishra, 'South Asia's Quest for Identity and SARC', India Quarterly, Vol.XL, Nos. 3 & 4, July-December, 1984, p. 316.

16. Mohammad Shamsul Haque, International Politics : A Third World -Perspective;: Sterling Publishing. Pvt. Ltd., New Delhi, 1987, pp. 48-49.

17. Gamani Corea, 'Regional co-operation in South Asia: Perspectives and Prospects; South Asia Journal, Vol.l, No. l (1987), p. 2.

18. S.D. Muni, "South Asian Association for Regional Co-operation", International Asian-forum, Vol. 18, No. 3-4, November 1987, p. 237.

19. Norman D. Palmer, The New Regionalism in Asia and the Pacific (Lexington: Books Co.,1991), p. 73.

20. Jean Gottmann, " Geography and International Relations", in W.A. Dauglas Jackson (ed.), Politics and Geographic Relationship (Englewood Cliffs, N.J. Princeton Hall, 1964), pp. 3-4.

21. Joseph S. Nye, Peace in Parts: Integration and Conflict in Regional Organization, (New York: University Press of America, 1987), pp. 3-4.

22. Joseph S. Nye, op. cit., p. 3.

23. Ellen Fray Wauters, "The Prospects for Regionalismin World Affairs", in Richard Fald and Cyril Black (eds.), The Future of the International Legal Order, Vol.1 (Princeton N.J.: Princeton University Press, 1969), p. 18. See also Joseph S. Nye, op.cit., p. 8.

24. Thomas Frank, "Who Killed Article 2(4)"?, American Journal of International Law (AJIL), (Washington D.C.), Vol. 64 (1970), p. 832.

25. For details, see Bruce M. Russett, International Regions and International System: A study of Political Ecology (Chicago, 1967), Chapter I, II.

26. See Alf. Ross, Constitution of the United Nations: Analysis of Structure and Fuction (New York, 1950), p. 166.

27. Article 53(1) of the UN Charter, reads in part as follows: the Security Council shall, where appropriate, utilise such

regional arrangement or agencies for enforcement action under its authority...".

28. See Norman Bentwich and Andrew Martin, A Commentary on the Charter of The United Nations (London, 1951), p. 100.

29. Joseph S. Nye, ed. International Regionalism: Readings (Boston, Mass, 1968), pp. 5-15.

30. See, E.N. Van Kleffens, 'Regionalism and Regional Pacts". American: Journal of International Law (AJIL), (Washington D.C.) Vol. 43, Oct. 1949, p. 668.

31. N.J. Padelford and C.A. Lincoln, International Politics (New York, 1954), p. 609.

32. See J.S. Nye, Peace in Parts: Integration and Conflict in Regional Organization (Boston, 1971), p. 5.

33. See Lynn Miller, "The prospects for order through Regional Security" in Richard Falk and Cyril E. Block, ed., The Future of International Legal Order (Princeton University Press), Vol. 1, p. 572.

34. Ibid, pp. 572-73.

35. Debendra Kumar Das (ed.); 'SAARC' Regional Co-operation and Development; Perspectives, Problems, Politics'; pp. 21-22.

36. Dr. V.R. Panchamukhi has advocated that if development paradigm in each country is cohesen with the objectives of serving the basic needs of the people in much better way than what is done in the past, and if technologies and baskets of goods and services at macro-level are chosen in such a manner as to be relevant to the imperatives of sub-region specific endowments, the potential of regional co-operation would be larger. For detail, see "Regional Co-operation and development" Paper presented for workshop at SAARC Scenario held at Kathmandu, Nepal, March 21-22, 1991.

37. For more elaborating and comprehensive term on the subject, see Gomulka, Stanislaw; Growth, Innovation and Reform in Eastern Europe, University of Wisconsin Press,

1986, Gorbachev, MIchail Perstroika: New thinking for our country and the World, Collins, London, 1987, and Kozminski, Andrzej K., "Reforming Socialist Economy: Common Dilemmas", Paper presented at the International Conference on 'New Frontiers in Economic Policy', Poland, 5-10 Oct., 1987, Management Science, Warsaw.

38. Das, Debendra K. : Inflation in Indian economy under Five Year Plans, Deep & Deep publications; New Delhi, 198/, p. 109.

39. Das Debendra K. : "Global Trade confrontations : Issues and challenges before SAARC in Ninties", The Indian Economic Association, Seventy-third conference, Volume, December 1990, pp. 41-52.

40. Panchamukhi, V.R., "World Economy in the Nineties: Issues in Sustainable Growth", C.N. Vakil Memorial Lecture delivered at 73rd Annual Conference of the, Indian Economic Association, held in Muzaffarpur, Dec. 28-30, 1990.

41. Sarkar, Subhash Chandra, "Anatomy of Aid", Young India Vol. 7, No. 6, March 19, 1991.

42. Mr. Ryutaro Hashimoto, the Finance Minister of Japan anticipated serious consequences of this tendency and drawn the grouping need for funds to rebuild East Germany to finance transition to market economies in the Eastern Europe and to reconstruct the Middle East at the Annual Meeting of Chairman of the Largest Commercial Banks at Osaka. He suggested that industrial countries should voluntarily loan the new special drawing right back to IMF for augmenting its ability to lead the needy countries; The Times of India, 7 June, 1991.

43. L.L. Mehrotra, H.S. Chopra, Gert W. Kueck (ed.) International Seminar 'SAARC 2000 and Beyond" 'Costs and Benefits of Regional Co-operation in South Asia' by Arif A. Waquif; Omega Scientific Publication of India; p. 131.

44. Sabyasachi Roy, 'Regional co-operation among SAARC countries'; Debendra Das (ed.) "SAARC: Regional co-

operation and Development" p. 100.

45. R.A. Rao, "India's opportunity for Regional co-operation in Technology Transfer among South Asian Countries", in K. Satya Murty (Ed.), South Asian Regional co-operation (1982), p. 132, Institute of Asian-Studies, Hyderabad.

46. op.cit., p. 132.

47. B. Satyanarayan, "Regional Co-operation Among SAARC Countries", in Debendra Kumar Das (ed.), 'SAARC: Regional Co-operation and Development', p. 77.

48. S.D. Muni and Anuradha Muni, 'Regional Co-operation in South Asia', p. 6.

49. Edgar S. Furniss, "A Rexamination of Regional Arrangements", Journal of International Affairs, IX (1955), p. 86.

# 2

# Formation of SAARC: Background

South Asia inhabitating one-fifth of the humanity the poorest belt of the world. The region covers only 3.3% of the world's land area and has less than 1% of the world's natural resources. The problem is compounded by a high rate of population growth and chronic food deficiencies in most of the countries. The countries of the South Asia region have been beset with morbit inter-state relations and complex regional and geo-political environment. The consequence had been the transformation of South Asia into a 'region of mistrust' where mutual tension, misperception and occasional hostilities have taken precedence over the possibilities of meaningful positive interaction and co-operation. Under these circumstances, the regional policy behaviour of states tend to be determined by often directed against each other[1].

South Asian countries have over history passed through intense experience of cultural absorptions, political expansions and break-ups, social turmoil and tranquility and economic need and affluence. Being shaped by these complex, incompatible and at times, even antagonistics experience, South Asian States and problems reflect a dynamic and persistence co-existance of discord and understanding, competition and convergence and conflict and collaboration in their mutual intaractions. Many analysts have not been able to grasp this Mistique fully and have tended to point a negative picture of South Asian reality encompassing wars, tensions, misunderstanding, divergence and antagonisms. Though negative aspects appear to dominate in South Asia, there are positive tendencies and creative impulses which are also rooted in history. It is, therefore necessary to examine the roots of conflicts as well as co-operated in South Asia in order not only to understand the past, comprehend the present, but also to project, and if possible, to influence the future in this regard[2].

The South Asian regional sub-system consists of seven states - Bangladesh, Bhutan, India, Maldives, Nepal, Pakistan and Srilanka. The subcontinent of India is a distinct geographical entity and consists of most of the South Asian States. Though Srilanka and Maldives are separated from the subcontinent by not too distant stretches of sea, they are tied to the South Asian system on other ground; a common civilizational heritage, religious and linguistic affinities. Past dominance by the British, either direct or indirect, provided yet another common experience conflict and tensions arose in South Asia over since the British departed, leaving many complicated and potential explosive issues unresolved. The situation was further complicated when the apprehensions generated not only included the leading states of the region to opt for divergent paths.

Generally, at the macro level, the South Asian countries approach to global issues of economic and military nature on the basis of non-aligned and 'independent' policies. The South Asian countries had in the past and still has a more or less non-aligned and independent approach to superpower rivalry and conflicts, the nuclear and conventional arms race between the great powers, the implications of North-South conflict, etc. But at the micro level regional discords and narrow national susceptibilities nourish divergences among the regional states. This suggests that global threat perceptions are subordinate to the intra-regional and national concerns in the South Asian region.

## Crucial Factors in Inter-State Relations in South Asia

South Asia as a region stands distinctly due to its geography, history, economy and culture. Most of the countries of the region share a colonial history. The region maintains a distinct cultural unity because of common religions and languages. Poverty, population, unemployment and slow economic growth rates are the common problems of South Asia. Nearly one billion population of these seven countries now comparising South Asia Association for Regional co-operation (SAARC)[3]. India, the core country in South Asia has 72 percent of regions area and 77 percent of its population and generates 78 percent of the GNP. This region has the singular misfortune of being the only area of without any form of regional co-operation[4], which could help moderate frictions arising out short term economic interests and encourage trade, industrial and technological ties among the seven countries.

There are some crucial factors influencing Inter-state relations in South Asia are as follows :

### (i) Colonial Legacy

Almost all the South Asian nations like India, Pakistan, Bangladesh and Srilanka had to experience the regourous impact of British colonialism. More or less the economy of South Asia became an appendage of the British economy.

A major offshoot of British imperialism in South Asia was the growing bitterness and distrust between the core-nation India and other peripheral nations, especially Pakistan, Bangladesh and Nepal. Therefore, with independence most of these nations planned their economies and trade patterns in isolation from one another. Because of such an unnatural diversion of the intra-regional trade in South Asia, the external economic relations of the regional states have become more or less competitive at the global level and quite negligible at the regional level, while looping at the statistics of intra-regional trade in South Asia, which comes down to less than one percent of the entire foreign trade of the region, one cannot resist the'temptation of suggesting that the negative role played by British imperialism has retarted the intra-regional trade in this region.

### ii) The Problems of Immigrants

The other socio-economic factor which has proved to be a major variable in the intra-regional relations in South Asia, is the process of immigration by the people of one country to another during the heyday of British rule in search of better living conditions. Moreover, with the departure of the British, when the sub-continent was partitioned, millions of people belonging to the Hindu and Muslim communities, were uprooted from their threats and had to be rehabilitated either in India or Pakistan. The herculean task of resettling such a vast multitude to human beings and the recovery of claims made by refugees from both countries resulted in a lot of misunderstanding and mutual discord between India and Pakistan. Primarily speaking, the intra-regional relations in South Asia are largely determined by the attitude of both India and Pakistan towards each other and their stand major regional and international issues.

During the colonial era, a large number of Indian workers moved to the neighbouring countries Burma (now Myanmar) and Srilanka, to serve in British owned industries and plantations. These immigrant Indians having improved their lot by hard work, did not like to return to their homeland even after the withdrawal of the British colonial power and the granting of formal independence to its colonies. But they soon became eyesores to the new indigenous leaders in both Srilanka and Burma. They called for the repartition of these peoples of Indian origin on the plea that their national economies could not afford to absorb so many aliens. On the other hand, India, with its mounting pressure of population and poor state of economy, could not afford to take back all these people. Naturally, this problem became a major bottleneck between the major South Asian nations and other peripheral ones like Srilanka and Burma.

## (iii) Ethno - Religious Conflicts

Religion plays a very important role in South Asian Politics. The sub-continent had to be partitioned on the basis of religions with India becoming pre-dominantly Hindu and Pakistan and subsequently, Bangladesh, predominantly Muslim countries[5]. Religion as a national symbol is concerned, it is clear that Pakistan and Bangladesh have taken it to the extreme. Islam serves as a sort of national identity for the ruling elites of both these states. The Pakistanis or Bangladeshies feel greatly concerned whenever there is any large-scale killing of Muslims in a communal riot in India. Similarly, the ruling elites in India project a sort of moral responsibility to protect the interest of the Hindu minority in both Pakistan and Bangladesh. Even at times some strong cases of anti-Hindu agitation in Srilanka have had their simultaneous reaction in India.

From ethnic point of views South Asia is one of the great melting pots of the world and its racial diversity perhaps the most complex to be found anywhere outside Africa[6]. There are six main religions, viz, Islam, Hinduism, Sikhism, Christianity, Buddhism and Jainism, hundreds of languages (including local dialects) and scores of ethnical groups subdivided into countless ethnical tribes. All religious, linguistic and ethnic loyalties run deep and religion played great role in shaping the nation-state system in the region while political boundaries of most of the state follow linguistic and ethnical boundaries. And in some cases, ethno-religious problem has been convinced or abetted from across the border with political motive.

Much more disturbing is, however, the spectre of communal violence that has escalated fresh in recent time.

Almost all the countries of the region are multi-religious and each has religious minority big or small. Although, there are deliberate, some times inadvertant discrimination against some minority community in some of the countries.

### (iv) Role of Language

The relevance of language in the intra-regional relations in South Asia lies in the fact that two major states, a number of languages are either spoken or understood in more than one country in the region. For instance, Urdu is spoken by a large number of North Indians and by a considerable number of people in South India, especially in the areas of the old Princely State of Hyderabad. In Pakistan, Urdu is recognized as the official language. Bengali is the official language of Bangladesh and is one of the regional language of India. Nepali, is the official language of Nepal, is largely spoken in the Darjeeling district of West Bengal in India. Tamil, one of the regional language in India, has been recognized also in Srilanka as a second language. Because of the colonial legacy, the elites in South Asia understand and speak English.

Because of the overlapping of some languages in the South Asian states, one often notices concern of the leaders of one nation for the recognition and upliftment of a particular language in the neighbouring country, provided that it is also largely spoken or used as official language in their own country. To cite the case of Pakistan, because of the fact that Urdu has been recognized as its official language, its ruling elites have always supported any move for its upliftment in India. Again, mainly because Bengali is spoken by a large segment of the Indian population, its leaders used to support the people of East Bengal, in undivided Pakistan, in their movement for the official recognition of Bengali as a national language.

Although the Government of India has not expressed any overt sympathy on the status and grievances of the Tamil minority in Srilanka, by and large, the people of Tamilnadu have been largely concerned at the discrimination and unfair treatment meted out to the Indian Tamils in Srilanka. The process of granting Srilanka citizenship to some of them and repatriating the rest to India has been unfortunately very slow and has remained a major battleneck in Indo-Srilanka relations.

Another instance of language playing a negative role in the intra-regional relations in South Asia can be noted in Nepal's special concern for the protection of Nepali language in the Darjeeling district of West Bengal, even though it falls within the exclusive domestic jurisdiction of India. However, such a negative pull can be converted into a positive force, provided the leaders of the region, while looking back to a common linguistic culture, join hands in certain co-operative ventures[7].

### (v) Bilateral Issues

Indeed South Asia continues to be bedevilled by a host of outstanding bilateral issues of both retrospective and prospective nature. The issues are obviously between India and most of the other countries in the region. Most of the bilateral issues are chronic in nature and remain unresolved for a long time, and with pass age of time new complications are added making them more difficult to be resolved.

Indo-Pakistan relations continue to pose the gravest threat to peace and stability in South Asia. The major issues that led to the armed conflict between these countries Kashmir thrice before, still remain unresolved the Kashmir problem remaining the central one. The issue drags on for four decades with no resolution of the question of self-determination of the people of Kashmir. Other irritants included the issue of US arms supply to Pakistan. The nuclear debate has added a new dimension to Indo-Pakistan dispute.

The most serious problems between India and Bangladesh was one on constructing of Farakha Barrage by which India had already done an "irrepairable damage" to life and economy of Bangladesh. Negotiation started on sharing of Ganges water after the barrage was commissioned in early 1975. The land border agreement of 1974 remains major irritant because after 13 years of agreement it is yet to be ratified by India. India was to provide Tinbigha corridor to a Bangladesh enclave.

Nepal's problem with India essentially centres round a strong Nepalese desire "for the projection of Nepal's independent indentity". The Nepalese monarchy assidously maintained Nepalese independence of actions (as was reflected in her signing a friendship treaty with her) and concluding also a boundary agreement with her) and Nepal began gradually to move out from under Indian's domination in foreign relations. That portends a phase of misunderstanding and bitterness between the two countries. Nepal remains suspicious because of its overwhelming pendence on trade and transit with India. India also is constantly worried of Nepal's tilt towards China, while Nepal does not like that Nepalese political activists receive supports from India. Nepal's dismay of India is be due to India's non-acceptance of Nepal's declaration iling it a 'zone of peace'.

Bhutan's primary problem, still both internally and externally, is one of "establishing its own personality as a nation". Bhutan's relation with India is threatened by the cross-country implication of the conditions of Bhutias living in Sikkim and parts of Northern Bengal[8]. Both, Nepal and Bhutan - the two landlocked countries of South Asia are keen to have access to sea through multi-lateral approaches partly to escape from deep dependence on India. Though, in a low key way it also supports Nepal's 'Zone of Peace'.

### (vi) Dominant Position of India

The most important characteristic of the South Asia region is its Indo-centric nature. By its big size, resources and technological base, India is a colossus, almost three times bigger than all its South Asian neighbour put together and with ambitions for a hegemonic role to match. This naturally created an apprehension that any regional association of the countries of South of the Himalayas would be dominated. by India. This fear was confirmed by the experience of the smaller neighbours which has seen that in all disputed issues, India did not proceed on.the basis of recognised principles on international conduct, but tried to dictate from a position of strength. Furthermore, India's diplomatic stance in dealing with non-regional powers left little doubt that it expected them to pay head to its dominant position in subcontinental affairs[9].

India is central to the whole region. This is only so in terms of India's geographical location contiguous boundries with neighbours, but with respect socio-cultural identities and experiences of historical and political evolution, commonalities in South Asia are mostly bilateral between India and each of the neighbouring countries separately and individually. There is a bit of India in every other countries of South Asia. All the South Asian neighbours of India have only one thing in common amongst themselves and that is India. As a political corallary of the fear of domination, South Asian countries reiterated the respect for the principles of "sovereign equality, territorial integrity, political independence, non-interference in interal affairs" in their mutual dealings.

### (vii) Common Defence System

As fact stand, South Asia is the least developed region of the world. The countries of the region have developed no common political institutions, judicial bodies or security machinery. The vacuum created by the withdrawal of the British power has not been in any way filled by the countries of the region.

South Asia as a region cannot be developed on the kind of status quo. There are outstanding questions between India and Pakistan, which are yet to be resolved. The demand for Pakistan continues to bedevil the relations between Pakistan and Afghanistan. The question of Indian immigrants in Srilanka and Burma, though considerably cased, has brought about immense harm to intra-regional understanding. There are other innumerable problems. But it may be easier to solve them all against the wider background of the region than taking them up individually on the basis of any bilateral negotiations. A large country like India may have to make some sacrifices in the process settling these problems, but the region as a whole is definitely bound to emerge stronger in world affairs, and what it is to the advantage of the region will definitely be of advantage to India[10].

## Involvement of the Great Powers in South Asia

## The U.S. Policies in Indian Subcontinent

The US policy towards South Asia has always been a component but not so much important one of its global policy. As a result, US South Asia policy often fluctuated, changed and reversed depending on its other priorities and changes in its overall policy in international arena[11].

With the partition of the sub-continent into two separate states of India and Pakistan, there developed lot of mutual conflict and disharmony between the two. By keeping in tune with its global policy of supporting the weaker side in case of regional dispute, decided to back the Pakistanis in their offensive postures against India.

US basic objectives and interests in South Asia are subservient to its global objectives. These can be summed up as follows : increasing the military capacity, strenghening the military alliances, countering the spread of communist movement and finally, its opening to communist China. In terms of real performance to fulfill the above objectives, it can be submitted that although American succeeded partly, by and large, it has been disillusioned with the new international trends in this region and elsewhere[12].

US interests in South Asia are largely because of its location in the vicinity of two strategic regions of the world - the Gulf and South East Asia. It being located near two strategic areas like the Middle East and South East Asia.

## Soviet Union and South Asia

Soviet Union was directly involved in the intra-regional affairs in South Asia in the mid-fifties and this reached its high watermark in the Tashkent Declaration of 1966. Incidently, on the one hand, it had a growing rivalry with United States at the global level and an ideological dispute with communist China. On the other hand, on the South Asian platform, one notices the Indo-Pak dispute over Kashmir and India's hostile relations with China. Naturally such an interplay of global and regional factors brought Soviet Union closer to India. However, the Soviet could not afford to ignore their basic interests in other parts of South Asia and sometimes provided them with sizable economic and technical aids.

Because of its own economic prosparity, the Soviet Union is in a position to provide major assistance to the developing nations of South Asia. In fact, it is already doing so by economic assistance and technical knowhow to a number of projects undertaken by these nations. Even in terms of military hardware and strategic weapons, it is in a position to provide substantial help. All these factors have increased the bargaining capacity of the Soviets in this part of the world.

## Chinese Policy in South Asia

China is the third major global power directly involved in the intra-regional affairs in South Asia. When Indo-Pak hostilities started on a large scale soon after partition, the Communist leadership in China decided to capitalize on the difference. China and Pakistan have therefore supported each other in the international forums. Islamabad still holds a key position in China's security calculations. The all weather road between China and Pakistan occupied Kashmir, as mentioned earlier, has made the Indian ocean accessible to the former.

The search for leadership in the developing world is another aim of China. Keeping in tune with such a global objectives, it has supported insurgent in India and Nepal. It has even provided necessary training and weapons to group of Mizo and Naga rebels. It has also inspired the Naxalite Movement in India.

Being a major supplier of sophisticated weapons and economic aid to Pakistan, its relationship with India has more or less remained unsure. Moreover, because of its "carrot and stick" policy in Nepal, the ruling elites in Kathmandu have gone ahead to project an anti-Indian image in their foreign policy. Because of China's presence in this region, the other two global powers have naturally joined the race and thereby converted the subcontinent into a hot-bed of big power rivalries[13].

## Japan's Role in South Asia

Japan is a leading economic and trade partner for South Asia. In 1988 more than 10 percent of South Asia exports were directed towards Japan while over 11 percent of the region's imports came from this country alone. The balance, as expected is of course in favour of Japan which had $ 1.8 billion worth of trade surplus with South Asia. South Asia's trade deficit with Japan indeed about a quarter the region's deficit with the industrialized countries. Needless to mention, trade balance with Japan is negative for all the South Asian countries, the ration of value of import of these countries being the most cases many times that of exports.

In terms of economic aid, however, South Asia appears to be a much more important region from the view point of Japan. The role of Japan as a "donor superpowers because critical in this context". Japan's new international responsibility as it includes help establish global peace, cannot confined to extending money in the name of economic assistance irrespective of developments in the political arena.

Referring to tensions between India and Pakistan over the disputed territory of Kashmir, the Japanese Prime Minister urged India and Pakistan to "exercise self-restraint and try to resolve the issue peacefully through talk's. Tokyo's continued economic assistance may indeed be used as an instrument of positive sanction to include such favourable developments in the region as cuts in defense budgets and other measures for reducing tensions, like use of dialogue instead of confrontation in interstate relations. Japan's aid has so far focused basically on large - scale projects which do contribute to the development of the recipient's infra-structure"[4].

## Efforts For Regional Co-operation in South Asia

The early recent attempt at building regional co-operation in South Asia needed be viewed within the framework of regionalism in the third world in general and Asia in particular. The early talk on Asian regionalism came from Japan and many in India and elsewhere were influenced by the Japanese slogan of "Asia for the Asians". The Japanese motivations, however, being imperialistic were exposed before and during the second world war as a result of their policies towards Burma, China and Korea[15].

The genesis of regional co-operation in South Asia can be traced to 1945 when Jawahar Lal Nehru had advocated the imperative need to establish a South Asian federation for unity, peace and progress in the region. But the serious attempts towards regionalism began after the advent of independence in Asia from the colonial rule in 1947. Several initiatives were taken into this direction. But there was a lack of clarity and precision about the region that was to be evolved into a viable grouping for common purposes as is evident from the geographical diversity and variation of the participating countries and from Nehru's speech itself.

> "We have not yet decided what the region of co-operation might be...., India is interested in several regions of Asia, whether all should be grouped together or separating, we do not know"[16].

General political conferences were one of the principal forums of regional association in which South and South East Asian countries have taken part during fifties. There have been three such conferences; the Asian Relation conference at New Delhi in 1947, the conference of Asian, Australian and Middle Eastern Nations on the Indonesia question at New Delhi in 1949, and the Asian-African conference at Bandung in 1955. South Asian delegates played prominent role at all the three meetings, and the regional co-operation was the central point in their opinions.

## The Asian Relations Conference (23rd March, 1947 2nd April, 1947)

The Asian Relations conference, which met in Delhi at 23rd March 1947 to 2 April, 1947, was the first of these conferences. It was a non-official gathering converted under the ouspicies of the Indian Council of World Affairs for the discussion of common Asian problems and Asia's positions in the Post war world. Prime Minister of India played a leading role in organizing the conference in response to a vague but wide spread feeling among the newly independent and soon to be independent nations of that such a meeting could serve a useful purpose at the time. Delegations from twentyeight countries attended[17], although it is probable that none of them could have defined exactly the reasons which brought them together. The conference agenda included National Freedom Movement in Asia, racial problems and inter-racial migration, cultural affairs, Agricultural and Industry[18]. No progress whatsoever, was made on the creation of a formal Asian Union, a project warmly responsed by some delegates[19].

The tone for the conference was set by Nehru in his inaugural speech. Four major points in his speech were the proclamation of Asia's arrival on the world secene, the stress on the need for Asian Unity, the need to avoid the expression of anti-western sentiments and the need for greater regional co-operation.

However, the conference started with a great deal of initial expression of enthusiasm. Srilanka's Bandarnaike saw in it the beginning of an Asian federation, while Burma's Aung San in his message urged the Asian countries to stand together in weal or weo[20]. Most other delegates expressed their great satisfaction at this sign of Asian resurgence and unity. The conference also ended on a hopeful note : The Asian Relations Organization was to be created with the subjectives of promoting Asian studies and greater co-operation among Asian countries and "between them and the rest of the world"[21].

In the end, the conference accomplished little to consequences. It gave rise to two new unofficial bodies, on institute of Asian Studies and An Asian Relations Organization, none of which has since played a conspicuous role. The intention of holding a second conference at Hangehow, China in 1949 failed to materialize.

### Conference on Indonesia: (New Delhi, 20 January 1949)

After Netherlands launched its second "police action" against the Indonesian Republic in December 1948, Prime Minister Jawaharlal Nehru, who had been aconsistent and outspoken apponent of Dutch policy in the archipelago, evoked on emergency conference of ninteen countries at New Delhi on 20 January 1949 to discuss the crisis. The conference of Asian, Australian and Middle Eastern nations on the Indonesian question met in January 1949. The conference on Indonesia unlike the earlier Asian governments and had official charter. It was also specially political in nature.

Nehru enunciated a three-fold task for the discussion in conference:

(i) to frame and submit reasonable proposals for the settlement of the Indonesian question:

(ii) to suggest lines of actions to the Security Council in case either party fails act according to its recommendations;

(iii) to devise machinery and procedure for the assembled governments to keep in touch with each other. Nehru also made an open appeal for regional integration; "we see creative and co-operative impulse seeking a new integration and new unity. New problems arise from day-to-day which in their implications, concern all of us of many of us"[22].

The conference adopted three resolutions: one, strongly criticising Dutch action and using effective UN action; second, agreeing that the representatives of the attending countries in the United Nations should consult among themselves on the issue of Indonesia; and third, asking the participating governments to "consult among themselves in order to explore ways and means of establishing suitable machinery... for promoting consultations and co-operation within the framework of the United Nations[23].

Interestingly, more than Nehru, it was now Carloe Romulo of the Philippines, who was interested in promoting the regional ideas. During the conference, Romulo urged the establishment of "a continuing machinery.... including a small permanent Secretariat in New Delhi, or may be Manila, to serve as a clearing house of information essential to concerted action by our various governments...." The conference on the Indonisian question had a definite influence on the eventual settlement of the Dutch - Indonesia dispute. Its resolution on the establishment or regional machinery, however, led to nothing.

## The Baguio Conference : (May 1950)

The Baguio conference, held in May 1950 was attended by India, Pakistan, Australia, Indonesia, Thailand and Srilanka. General co-operation in cultural fields was recommended in its resolutions.

When the Philippines took the initiative of Asian countries to consider matters of regional concern, India's response was at least half hearted and uneuthusiastic. India had earlier rejected the Australian attempt to form Pacific pact. While Australia was ready to go it alone with the US, Britain insisted that India should be included in such a conference and India insisted that the conference should concern itself with only non-military aspect of co-operation. The solution was ultimately found in the Colombo Plan on the one hand and the ANZUS on the other. The problem with Philippines initiative was that it was almost clear from the beginning that any such regional effort would be anti-communist in nature.

## Colombo Plan (1950)

The Colombo Plan for co-operative Economic Development in South and South East Asia was perhaps the best known of regional schemes for the promotion of economic progress in the area. It began in January 1950 as a British Commonwealth project, but soon expanded for beyond its original geographical scope. All the countries of South East Asia, except North Vietnam, were included among its membership.

The Colombo meeting had set up a consultative committee for surveying the needs of the area, assessing the resources and manner available in the region and providing an international framework within which the co-operative efforts for assisting the countries of the region could be developed. In the London meeting of the committee of September 1950, the plan was put through in the form of the adoption of the report of the committee which incorporated reports of individual country[24].

The distinctive feature of the Colombo Plan is its emphasis on regional co-operation regarding technical training to their partners in the plan among of the 15 countries, India with 266 awards comes fifth after the USA (2,356), UK (623), Australia (446) and Japan (305).

While the plan has achieved considerable result in one

sense, it is doubtful whether it can be compared with other regional plans. The former Indian Ambassador to the United States, G.K. Mehta, said about the plan, the most important feature of the Colombo Plan is that it is not a plan at all. It is not a blueprint of a regional development programme. The Colombo Plan is an arrangement international economic co-operation. It has no central organisations, no irksome rules of procedure, no head quarters and no permanent Secretariat"[25].

The US government had indeed attempted to help the growth of economic regionalism in the area when in 1955 it let be known that it was prepared to set aside a sum of $ 200 Million for projects in the region which would benefit a number of countries. The response, however, was not encouraging.

## The Bandung Conference (April 1955)

The attempts at regional co-operation, however, continued at other level of Bandung Conference, is usually regarded as the high point of an Afro-Asian attempt to develop agreed bases of policy and a common approach to their problems.

The Conference met in Bandung in April 1955. All initiatives with the exception of Central African Federation joined the conference. The conference released an agreed communique dealt with economic co-operation, cultural co-operation, human rights and self-determination, problems of dependent peoples and problems of world peace and co-operation. In the economic sphere, the conference agreed to the general need for economic co-operation in the region, of providing mutual technical assistance, of exchange of know how, of the establishment of regional training institutes, if possible of collective action to stablise raw material prices, of intra-regional trade fairs, collective bargaining with shipping lines, establishment of regional Banks, etc.[26], but the most crucial part of the communique was the demand that the UN should create the special United Nations Fund for Economic Development and divert more resources to the region.

From the point of view of establishing once and for all the new status of the Asian and African nations in international politics as their claim to a place in the counsels of the nations, Bandung must be put down as a resounding success. It brought the newly independent countries of Asia and Africa in close co-operation. It should be noted in discussing the Bandung conference that there was a difference between Nehru and other neutralists regard to the general tone of the conference. It is not surprising, therefore, that the Indian reaction to Bandung was not enthusiastic.

### Conference at Brioni (July 1956)

From India's viewpoint more meaningful was the conference at Brioni in 1956 among the leaders of the three nonaligned nations with any degree of similarity approach India, Yugoslavia and Egypt.

All the reports on the conference agreed that Nehru had played the moderating role. It is noted in the Fact on Files, "the conference.... produced no formalised neutralist bloc which was Nehru was said to have opposed[27]. The New York Times brought out an interesting aspect of the conference in an editorial, "Asia from their neutralist attitude, the three statement have little in common and each has separate and individual problems to meet. Tito is a communist, Nehru is a democratic socialist and Nasser the meeting with Nehru, head of one of the most popular countries of the world, meant undoubtedly an accertion of prestige and was exploited as such. It served to emphasise their independence of both East and West and to minimise the isolation into which they were isolating themselves. But to Nehru, the meeting could mean neither prestige nor profit, and it was he therefore, who put the brapes on whether larger ambitions the other two might have had[28].

### The New Delhi Conference (1961)

In September 1961, a conference of Asian Economic Planners in New Delhi again considered problems of regional co-operation. The direct purposes of the conference were more limited the establishment of an Asian Institute of Economic Development and a Regional Advisory Group on Economic Development and Planning. The conference succeeded in achieving the limited results envisaged, but wider co-operation, which was ably advocated by the ECAFE Secretariat in an elaborate note prepared for the occasion, was stalled by some members. "A typically cautious note was pounded by the representative of Srilanka, who while supporting the general idea of regional co-operation stated that it should not mean the colonial type of complementarity. A similar note was uttered by the representative of Pakistan[29].

A close analysis of these conferences reveals some important aspects of the early attempts at regionalism solving South Asian countries. Firstly, there was a lack of clarity and precision about the region that was to be evolved into a viable grouping for common purposes, as in evident from the geographical diversity and variations of the participating countries at these conferences, secondly, these attempts were dominated by the politico-strategic considerations on the one hand of military pacts and alliances, and on the other hand of decolonization and Asian resurgence. Economic aspects of co-operation figured in these conferences only casually and without such success[30].

From a functionalist viewpoint, these early attempts at regional co-operation in South Asia do not merit much attention. The participating countries were only vaguely aware that a regional co-operation approach to much of their economic and developmental strategy could be beneficial and mutually rewarding.

In the late 1970s, the group of scholars in the South Asian countries began to exchange ideas of possible lines of regional co-operation, with a focus on economic and social development. "In September 1978, their efforts were formalized when academic institutions in six South Asian countries agreed to set in motion a concerted and systematic programme of studies under a committee on studies for co-operation in Development in South Asia (CSCD)[31]. The scholars of the South Asian region held a number of meetings and made a number of proposals that helped to provide the kind of background analysis and information which proved to be useful to those who later worked out the details of the new organization under the direction of the Foreign Secretaries and Foreign Ministers of the South Asian States.

## Formation of SAARC: Bangladesh Proposal

In 1979, Late President Zia-Ur-Rahman of Bangladesh mooted the idea of South Asian regional co-operation. In his proposal he called for a summit meeting of the leaders of the seven South Asian countries, i.e., Bangladesh, Bhutan, Maldives, Nepal, Pakistan and Srilanka. The purpose of such summit was to "explore the possibilities of establishing a framework for regional co-operation". The imperatives for such a call by Bangladesh can be traced much to the, genuinely felt quest for collective self-reliance in terms of South-South co-operation and the ongoing North-South dialogue as the need for gaining additional leverage for smaller states of the region vis-a-vis India[32].

The President of Bangladesh was working on this Idea about three years back before giving it a concrete shape and announcing it. The issue was shared with the Indian leaders when he visited India in December 1977, and his visit followed a similar visit by Prime Minister Morarji Desai on April 15-17, 1979. It, however, could not be anticipated that the Janata rule in India was on its way out, subsequently when Mrs. Gandhi came back to power in January 1980, the Bangladesh leader approached her on the subject. In January 1978 during the visit of King Birendra of Nepal to Bangladesh, President Zia welcomed the King's call for close regional co-operation made by a month earlier[33]. He also visited Srilanka in November 1979 and talked with the President J.R. Jayawardene. Both the leaders decided to work on this idea on the basis ASEAN.

The proposal was promptly endorsed by Nepal, Srilanka, Maldives and Bhutan. But India and Pakistan had some reservations on this proposal. In India, Mrs. Gandhi came into power in 1980 after three years. She accepted the proposal in principle, but did not want to endorse it in toto. There were some reasons also not to endorse this proposal. India was isolated in the region on some of the vital world issues like Afghanistan, Cambodia and the Indian Ocean. India's position was contrary to that of its relations with Pakistan and Bangladesh were also not very satisfactory. It was also thought in India that the proposed regional forum would isolate India on global issues and contain India's position in South Asia.

Lack of enthusiasm for the Bangladesh proposal from Pakistan was based on different consideration. Pakistan, perhaps on erroneous perception felt that the move was prompted by India. Furthermore she viewed, that became of India's greater economic potential and scientific and technological capabilities, the attempt was to ensure regional market for Indian products. This, Pakistan thought, would lead to the consolidation and further strengthening of India's economic dominance with its consequent political implications in the region[34]. Accordingly, Pakistan become afraid of losing its political stance in the subcontinent of joining this move of regional co-operation, without resolving its bilateral issues with India, particularly that of Kashmir, to its advantage. Pakistan was also apprehensive that its deeper involvement with the South Asian region, which was to be a natural outcome of the Bangladesh proposal could weaken the credibility and drive of its policy option to cultivate and harness mutually profitable relations with the South-West Asian region in the emerging strategic and economic situation there.

The Indian and the Pakistani reservations were based upon their respective perceptions of national interests and how they were to be adversely affected by the suspected intentions and motives behind the Zia-Ur-Rahman's initiative there was, however, nothing apparently objectionable in the proposal that in essence called for regional harmony and co-operation aimed at economic development in the compelling regional and international contexts. Therefore, India and Pakistan could not outright reject the proposal either. They instead sought to modify it so as to accommodate their respective apprehensions and requirements. It was decided to keep the bilateral and politically controversial issues out of the purview of the foreign Secretaries meeting.

Bangladesh was entrusted with the responsibility of preparing the draft of a working paper which could be discussed at the first meeting of the foreign Secretaries. Bangladesh prepared and circulated the draft paper in November, 1980. It had three important features. First of all, the objectives of regional co-operation were defined in very wide terms. The scope of co-operation was not viewed as confined narrowly to economic matters, but as "promoting active co-operation among countries of the region on matters of common interest in the economic, social, cultural, technical and scientific as well as is such other fields as may be agreed upon...." Wider scope was envisaged not only in the areas of co-operation, but also in terms of geographical extent because one of the objectives identified in the draft was to "explore all avenues of closer co-operation between the countries of South Asia and the other regional and international organisations with similar aims and objectives".

Secondly, Bangladesh draft identified eleven specific areas of co-operation. They were considered as "non-political" and "non-controversial" items. The areas were shipping, Aviation, Tourism, Telecommunication, Meteorology, Agriculture and Rural Developments, Joint Ventures, Land transport, Trade (market promotion in selected countries), Science and Technology, Education and Culture".

Finally, the draft suggested various institutional and

organisational aspects of regional co-operation the emphasis was on a Summit of the heads of governments thought it was accepted that way for the Summit could be prepared by the meetings of foreign Secretaries and foreign ministers[35].

## First Meeting of Foreign Secretaries (Colombo, 21-23 April 1981)

At the invitation of the Government of the Democratic Socialist Republic of Srilanka, the Foreign Secretaries of Bangladesh, Bhutan, India, Maldives, Nepal, Pakistan and Srilanka, met in Colombo from April 21 to 23, 1981, in pursuance of the initiative taken by His Excellency President Zia-ur Rahman of establishing regional co-operation among the countries of South Asia. The Foreign Secretaries elected by acclamation Mr. W.T. Jayasinghe, Foreign Secretary of Srilanka as the Chairman of the meeting.

To the meeting the Foreign Secretaries agreed (a) the regional co-operation was necessary, desirable and beneficial; (b) the decision should be taken on the basis of unanimity; and "bilaterial and contentious issues should be exluded from their deliberations"; (c) that sach co-operation should be based on respect for the principles of sovereign equality, territorial integrity, political independence, non-interference in internal affairs of other states", (d) The regional co-operation was not to be a substitute for bilateral and multilateral co-operation but could compliment both; nor should it be inconsistent with bilateral and multilateral obligations.

Foreign Secretaries noted that the South Asian countries are co-operating with one another and with other developing countries in various international forums. They agreed that efforts should be made to strengthen this co-operation, particularly on matters of common interest.

To begin with, five specific areas of beneficial regional co-operation were identified at this meeting. Agriculture, Rural development, Telecommunications, Meteorology and health and Population. Five study groups, co-ordinated by Bangladesh, Srilanka, Pakistan, India and Nepal respectively, were instituted to make in-depth studies in order to review the existing arrangements, and assess the feasibility and scope for regional co-operation in the overall cost-benefit framework. They were also charged with suggesting ways and means for establishing and strengthening co-operation by identifying specified projects and spelling out appropriate modalities for implementing and monitoring the work programme.

It was also agreed to set up a committee of the whole to consider the possibilities of identifying further areas of co-operation. The committee of the whole held in Colombo from 31 August to 2 September identified the following areas of co-operation, Education and training, Cultural Exchange, Scientific and Technological co-operation in International Economic Negotiation and Mass Communications, Marine Pollution Control, Postal Services, Manpower Export co-orination and co-operation amongst Regional Planners, non-governmental organisations, Research and other Institutions.

The Foreign Secretaries agreed that Kathmandu, Nepal, will be the venue for their next meeting.

## Second Meeting of Foreign Secretaries, Kathmandu, (November 2-4-1981)

The meeting decided to convert Five Study Groups into working groups, the major task of which would be to draw up a comprehensive programme of action for co-operation in both the immediate and long term phase. The immediate Action programme would include- exchange of information, exchange of experts etc., organizations of seminars etc., the long terms Action programme would include, among others Assessement of needs and resources, preparation of specific projects. In addition to five areas already identified, the meeting identified three more areas of co-operation i.e., transport co-ordinated by Maldives, Postal Services co-ordinated by Bhutan and Scientific and Technological co-operation co-ordinated by Pakistan.

### Third Meeting of Foreign Sectretaries, Islamabad (August 7-9-1982)

The third meeting of foreign secretaries was held at Islamabad in August 1982. A notable step taken at this conference was the decision to hold meeting at Foreign Ministers level in New Delhi in the middle of 1983. Other decision were -

(a) Recommendations of the five working groups were endorsed.

(b) There study groups set up at the previous meeting were converted into working groups.

(c) An additional study group in the field of sports, art and culture was set up.

(d) Agreed that regular consultations should by the representatives of the countries of the as deemed appropriate, on matters of common relating to international economic issues".

(e) Decided to set up a committee of the whole under Chairmanship of Srilanka and prepared Integrated Programme of Action in agreed areas.

The committee of the whole, on which high officials of the seven countries were represented, met in Colombo, in January 1983, alongwith the heads of the eight working groups. Two categories of action programmes were identified for co-operation. Amongst short term programmes, these are the followings - Exchange of data, Exchange of Experts Services, Training and Research, Holding of regional seminars etc. The long term programmes are the establishment of regional institutions for training and research, creation of linkage among the existing national institutions of the seven countries and strengthening of infrastructure in such areas as postal services, telecommunications, railways etc., which would require capital investment by the participating countries. The committee of the whole recommended to redesignate the Working Groups as Technical Committee at Sectoral level and to constitute a Standing/ Review Committee at Regional level.

### Fourth Meeting of Foreign Secretaries – Dhaka (March 28-30, 1983)

The fourth meeting of the seven Foreign Secretaries was held in Dhaka in March 1983. In this meeting, it was agreed that the first meeting of Foreign Ministers of the seven countries would be held in New Delhi to be preceded by a preparatory meeting of Foreign Secretaries. Another important decision at this meeting was the endorsement of the Integrated Programme of Action as recommend by the committee of the whole. A Standing Committee was also decided to be constituted at the Foreign Secretaries level.

### Preparatory Meeting of Foreign Secretaries, New Delhi (July 28-29, 1983)

In this meeting Report at the Study Group on Sport, Arts and Culture was agreed and recommended for incorporation in Integrated programme of Action. There were provisions of financial contribution from South Asian Countries and external assistance. Additional areas of cooperation and adoption of Integrated Programme of Action were considered and adopted in this meeting. The text of the draft Declaration of SAARC was considered for approval.

During the Dhaka meeting of Foreign Secretaries, it was decided to hold the first ministerial meeting in Delhi in August 1983. Through these four meetings, foreign secretaries did considerable ground work on two major aspects of the regional cooperation move.

The first is the organisation aspect. It was agreed at the last meeting in Dhaka that they were progressively advancing towards a "framework" for structured regional co-operation in South Asia. By the fourth meeting, three to four tiers of organisational structure had become identifiable. A summit meeting of the South Asian heads of governments may be mentioned as the first. The second tier in descending order was of course the ministerial meeting which was scheduled to have its session in New Delhi in August 1983. At the third tier was the foreign secretaries meetings. The four meetings held at this level were assisted by the two committees of the whole which met on two occasions under Srilanka's Chairmanship in September 1981 and January 1983 respectively. In pursuance of the decisions of the January 1983. Meeting of the committee of whole the Dhaka meeting decided to entrust the responsibility of the foreign Secretaries meeting and the committee of the whole put together to one unit redesignated as "Standing/Review Committee" and constituted by foreign Secretaries. This was to meet once in a year for "co-ordinating and monitoring the Integrated Programme of Action". This standing committee was to work under the overall policy guidelines given at the ministerial level. The foreign Secretaries have also been authorized to set up Action Committees in Case of such projects which involved more than two but not all the countries of the region.

And lastly, at the fourth level were the "technical committee", to be manned by officials of all the member countries and assigned to do the work done in the past two years by the working groups and study groups on identified and agreed areas of co-operation. The terms of reference of the 'technical committee" were also defined. Though these institutional levels and structures have been identified and put into operation, it would be safe to assume the organizational aspect was still in the process of evolution and may undergo further additions and transformations.

The second important aspect of the ground work done by the meetings of the foreign Secretaries was the identification of the areas for co-operation preparation an Integrated Programme of Action. Out of the eleven, areas, namely, agriculture, rural development, telecommunication, meteorology and health and population were identified and agreed at the Colombo meeting of foreign Secretarues. To these five, three more namely transport, Postal service and scientific and technological field were added at the second meeting in

Kathmandu. The Islamabad meeting added yet another field i.e. of sports, arts and cultures. At the Islamabad meeting the foreign Secretaries also agreed to hold regular consultations "by the representatives of the countries of the region, as deemed appropriate on international economic issues of common interest.

Besides finalising technical matters, the four meetings of the foreign Secretaries also revealed the approaches of the member countries towards the pace and scope of the regional co-operation move initiated by Bangladesh. The two most enthusiastic countries who wanted a faster pace i.e. an early summit meeting and a wider; scope were Bangladesh and Srilanka. Nepal, Bhutan and Maldives went along with these two countries both on the question of scope and pace, though they were less pronounced and forthcoming. As noted earlier, both India and Pakistan preferred a slow and cautions approach. Both were totally opposed to the faster face in convening the summit meeting. Regarding the scope of co-operation, whereas India was willing to include more area, Pakistan consistently maintained a go slow tactics.

However, the representatives of the two countries differed from one another in their styles of pursuing their respective lines, Pakistan appeared to be vigorously active, assertive its diplomatic offensive in toning down the enthusiasm of Srilanka and Bangladesh, India could play its card skillfully by starting its position firmly appearing to be obstructive India proposed a whole range of new areas to be included for co-operative activity. It succeeded in getting postponed to the next meeting the consideration about the convening of the foreign ministers meeting.

## First Meeting of Foreign Ministers, New Delhi (August 1-2, 1983)

The Foreign Ministers of the seven countries of the region formally meet for the first time in New Delhi on August 1-2, 1983. The meeting of the Foreign Ministers, the first of its kind over held at the political level to discuss regional co-operation anong South Asian partners is by all accounts, a significant development in this part of the world in recent times. The Declaration on South Asian Regional co-operation issued at this meeting underlined the collective resolve of the respective countries to "pursue actively" the goal of regional co-operation. The objectives spelt out in the declaration included inter alia, promotion of the welfare of the peoples of South Asia: acceleration of the economic growth, social progress and cultural development in the region; strengthening of collective self-reliance among the countries of the 'region, promotion of active collaboration and mutual assistance in economic, social, cultural and scientific fields: and co-operation among themselves in international forums on matters of common interest.

The Integrated Programme of Action was also launched formally at this meeting. Elaborate guidelines were, laid down for institutional and financial arrangements. Technical committees were set up in selected areas of co-operation to formulate programme of action; implementation and co-ordinate the concerned programmes at the sectorail level; and monitor the progress of implementation.

Provisions was also made for instituting Action Committees in case of projects involved more than two countries but not all the countries of the region. At the regional level, a standing committee at the level of foreign Secretaries, scheduled to meet at least once a year, was constituted; (1) to approve the projects including the modalities of financing; (2) to determine intersectoral priorities and overall co-ordination of Programme of Action; (3) to mobilise regional and external sources; and (4) to identify new areas of co-operation.

As for the financial arrangements, it was decided that the participation of each country in the financial courts of the programme would be voluntary. However, certain guidelines were laid down for the apportionment of the costs.

Provision was also made for recourse to external assistnace from appropriate sources, should the funds mobilized from within the region prove inadequate. It was also agreed that Foreign Ministers would meet once a year to review the progress of South Asian Regional co-operation.

### First Session of the Standing Committee, New Delhi (February 27-28, 1984)

The Foreign Secretaries meet for the first time as members of the permanent standing committee set up in August 1983. The standing committee examined reports of the nine Technical Committees which had held their meetings in the preceding six months. The committee also reviewed the world economic situation and urged that the proposal put forward by the Non-Aligned Movement and the Group of 77 at various forums should be actively persuade. It was also agreed that "all South Asian countries would work together in the appropriate international forums to promote the foregoing objectives".

### Second Session of the Standing Committee, Male (July 7-8, 1984)

This meeting, held prior to the Foreign Ministers' meeting to be held on 10-11 July, basically worked on two items (1) to drafted a Joint Communique for the Foreign Ministers meeting and (2) Prepared a report containing recommendations for strengthening and streamlining the institutions, to be submitted to the Foreign Ministers. The Report included following two recommendations by Pakistan that SAARC should draw up a calendar of its activities on yearly basis in advance on the pattern on UN calendar and Pakistan would convene a meeting of civil aviation officials and airline experts from member countries for improving the air transportation system in the region.

### Second Meeting of Foreign Ministers, Male, (July 10-11, 1984)

The Standing Committee's recommendations were

considered and endorsed by this committee. The Foreign Ministers felt that considerable progress had been achieved in implementing the Integrated Programme of Action in a relatively short time. The Foreign Ministers reviewed the current world economic situation. They expressed general disappointment at the fact that no appreciable progress was made by the developed countries in meeting the need of the developing countries. Dissatisfied with the situation regarding IDA-VII, they requested the Chairman to formally convey the concern of the South Asian countries to the leaders of the industrialized countries and in particular to the Prime Minister of Japan. They also agreed to recommendation to their heads of the governments, the convening of the First Summit meeting in Dhaka in the last quarter of 1985.

### Third Session of the Standing Committee, Male (February 5-7, 1985)

This meeting was convene to review the progress made in implementing the programme of action in different areas of co-operation and to intimate the preparatory process for the first ever summit of the SAARC to be held in Dhaka in December, 1985. The meeting expressed satisfaction over the progress made in the implementation of various projects in cultural, economic and technical fields, specially ever the regional centres being set up for promoting research and co-ordination. Regarding the summit, the Foreign Secretary of Maldives was entrusted with the task of revising the draft of the charter to be adopted by the summit.

### Fourth Session of the Standing Committee - Thimpu (May 10-11, 1985)

The meeting was held to prepare for the Ministerial conference to be held on 13-14 May. In the Standing committee meeting the SAARC faced its first crisis when Srilanka, objecting to a statement by India on Tamil problem made earlier by the Indian Minister of State for External Affairs, decided to boycott the conference. This was the first time when bilateral political dispute affected SAARC proceedings, revealing that the regional co-operation cannot be totally isolated from bilateral tensions. The Foreign Secretaries meeting was held without Srilanka's participation. It however ended its boycott on President Zia's mediation and attended the ensuing foreign Ministers conference.

## Third Meeting of Foreign Ministers - Thimpu (May 13-14, 1985)

The purpose of this meeting, besides reviewing the progress made, was to initiate arrangements for the SAARC 1985 Summit, and to consider the Draft Declaration and Draft charter to be issued at the meeting. The meeting recommended that the Summit meeting be held on 7-8 December 1985. They completed the draft charter which will formally be adopted at Dhaka, to institutionalize the process of regional co-operation.

During fourth meeting of Foreign Ministers of South Asian States in 1983 at Delhi, participants announced that the 'South Asian Association for Regional co-operation (SAARC) are launched.

After the formation of SAARC, there were mixed reaction in the region. While generally, the national dailies welcomed the regional association they were not certain if this could successfully achieve the goal of regional co-operation and friendship given the contrary relationships between some of the States in the region. It was being observed that some of these countries are even experiencing destabilisation as a result of terrorist activities, assassinations and insurgency aided and abetted by foreign sources. As to, who is playing what role remains a guessing game. But for making SAARC a success, pragmatic and unbiased approach is needed not only by India but all the members of SAARC.

The formation of SAARC in general terms is welcomed. However, it is also observed SAARC, like all other new born, perhaps would have to go through a period of teething trouble. But anyone could be greatly reduced if the seven member were to subject themselves to a period of a self-imposed moratorium on raising bilateral issues involving SAARC members[36].

The Indian Express (New Delhi) said that "the historicity of the events is self-evident, so is the need to protect and nourish the association to enable it to play the role chartered for it. Indeed, although bilateral problems fall outside the charter of SAARC, an overall umbrella of goodwill and co-operation can make them so much easier of solution[37]. All this of course assumes the availability and display of the necessary political will and purpose. One Chandigarh Daily commented that by creation of SAARC, 'mistrust cannot be removed overnight that creation inhibitions can be overcome and Dhaka Summit seems to have achieved this limited aim[38].

The SAARC Summit was also welcomed with varying notes in the other South Asian countries. One leading daily of Pakistan described it as a new era in South Asia'. It declared that the Dhaka Summit was certainly a high point in the new mood and spirit and reflected in the process of South Asian co-operation set in motion in 198l.

It however, pointed out that a lot will "depend on Whether the member nations will show the wisdom and prudence to take advantage of the goodwill and understanding generated by the new enterprise, for resolving "bilateral disputes and differences" and thereby creating a climate of regional peace and stability[39].

The Dhaka daily, Holiday commeding the role played by Bangladesh as the host of the Summit, stated that it was 'quite a diplomatic fact that Bangladesh could finally persuade leaders of six South Asian nations to assemble in Dhaka'to moot regional co-operation' aimed so much 'diversities plaguing South Asia'[40]. In conclusion, it stated that bilateral disputes within the region remain to be resolved.

The Bangladesh Times[41] lauded the new role played by

President Ershad and the initiatives that he had taken in convening the SAARC Summits in Dhaka.

The Rising Nepal[42] (Kathmandu) underscored the realistic approach of the SAARC leaders. Then it went on to add that the SAARC Summit opened a 'new chapter' in South Asia. The daily anticipated a better future for the region.

Commenting, presumably, in the context of the current situation in Srilanka, the Island State daily Sun[43] (Colombo) noted that, 'regional co-operation in the economic sphere is inevitably tied up with improved political relations among states'. 'The two process' it stated 'are complimentary' and 'need to be, reinforced if regional independence is to be made a reality'.

## Reactions Outside the Region

Among the major external powers, People's Republic of China, United States and Japan welcomed the formation of SAARC.

Chinese Premier Zhao Ziyang hailed the Dhaka Summit as 'as event of great significance in South Asian Region[44]. In a telegram to Bangladesh. President Ershad, he said, "China is delegated to see that, thanks to the joint efforts of the seven countries, gratifying process has been made in the South Asian Regional co-operation initiated by Bangladesh". SAARC, according to the Chinese Premier, was in the interest of the peoples of all the South Asian countries for it was deemed to bring peace in the region, Zhao wished the Summit a great success.

The US President Reagan, in his message to the Summit Chairman expressed his country's willingness to stand ready 'to provide appropriate assistance at your request in launching programmes of regional co-operation'[45].

The Soviets welcomed the first SAARC Summit of December 1985 as a positive development in South-South economic and other relations. Scholars at the India and South

Asia Department of the Institute of Oriental Studies made intense inquiries about SAARC'S regional co-operation portfolios, prospects of SAARC momentum packing up in 1987 after the establishment of Secretariat and the appointment of a Secretary General. South-South co-operation as one of the main pillars of a New International Economic order is very much on the agenda of Mikhail Gorbachev's foreign policy, both political and economic.

There is high appreciation in the Soviet Union of Prime Minister Rajiv Gandhi's efforts to help the Srilanka Government evolve a solution of the ethnic war that is tearing the Island republic apart. Equally high is the appreciation of Mr. Gandhi's desire to work jointly with Bangladesh and Nepal to develop the huge water resources of the eastern flank of the subcontinent.

However, the Soviets do not support Nepal's move to turn the Himalayan Kingdom into a "Zone of peace". The Soviets are generally supportive of large geo-political regions being declared zone of peace, they have refrained from lending support to the Pakistani concept of zone of peace in South Asia. The Soviets undoubtadly look at India as the leading light in SAARC, but Soviet scholars do stress the importance of India improving its relations with all its neighbours, including Pakistan.

In Tokyo, 1986, Mr. Yasuki Ono, head of the South- West Division in the Japanese Ministry of foreign affairs observed, "Japan has a very positive perception of SAARC. We consider the creation of SAARC to be one of the most constructive recent developments in Asia. We hope SAARC will grow rapidly as an instrument of regional co-operation. We shall be willing to commit funds for the project studies the seven SAARC countries have undertaken".

Mr. Ono, who was accompanied by two officials of the Foreign Ministry, disclosed that Japan would also be willing to help SAARC setup regional technical training institutes with funds and instructors. The Japanese institutes with funds and instructors. The Japanese Government had already written to the Indian foreign office offering to fund a SAARC training institute in New Delhi.

The United Nation's Secretary General Javier Perez de Cueller wished, "every success" to the formation of SAARC. In his message to the Summit Chairman, the UN Secretary General had declared in an optimistic note that the Summit will open 'a new era of progress' in South Asia and help reduce regional tensions. The UN Chief extended his sincere good wishes to President Ershad and other Heads of State and Government present in Dhaka for the historic conference of SAARC. He further stated that he had followed with satisfaction "the positive developments of this new regional organization in the past two years'. Indeed it was no coincidence that the venue of the conference was Dhaka in Bangladesh which had first proposed the idea of South Asian Regional co-operation.

## References

1. Nilufar Chaudhury, "Regional Approach to Security of Non-Aligned States: The Case of South Asia"; Bliss Journal, 1988, Vol. 9, No. 2; p. 243.
2. Jagdish Lal, 'Historical Background of establishment of SAARC', Third Concept, An International Journal of Ideas, December 1993, p. 24.
3. SAARC comprised of India, Pakistan, Bangladesh, Ceylon, Nepal, Maldives and Bhutan.
4. Other regional groupings besides security pacts are: ASEAN, OAU, EEC, OPEC, OAD, ANZUS, GCC and COMECON.
5. M. Abdul Hafiz, 'Regional Problems and Prospects for co-operation in South Asia', BIISS—Journal, Volume 8 N. 4, October 1987, p. 5.
6. Newsweek, 24 August 1987, p. 16.
7. P.K. Mishra, 'South Asia in International Politics' p. 5.
8. S.D. Muni, "Building Regionalism from Below" Asian Survey, Volume XXV, No. 4, p. 392.

9. Dr. Maqbool Ahemad Bhatty, "The future of SAARC", Regional Studies, Vol. 10, No. 1, Winter 1991-92, Quarterly Journal of the Institute of Regional Studies, Islamabad, p. 91.

10. S.P. Verma, "South Asia as a region; problems and prospects" South-Asian Survey, Vol. 1, No. 1, March 1976; pp. 25-26.

11. M. Abdul Hafiz, "South Asia's Security: Extra-regional inputs"; BIISS Journal, Vol. 10, No. 2, 1989, p. 135.

12. Robert Jackson, "The Great Powers and the Indian sub-continent", International Affairs (R.I.I.A London), January 1973, pp. 37-39. See also for a similar assessment, Leo E. Rose, The Super Powers in South Asia: A Geo-strategic Analysis", in Orbis (Pennsylvania), Vol. 2, 3; Summer, 1978, p. 395.

13. Pramod Kumar Mishra, "South Asia in International Politics", pp. 18-20.

14. Intekharuzzaman, "South Asia in the evolving inter-national context: the role of Japan", BIISS Journal, Vol. 11, No. 3, July 1990, pp. 283-309.

15. S.D. Muni and Anuradha Muni, 'Regional co-operation in South Asia', (New Delhi, National Publication, 1984).

16. Jawahar Lal Nehru, India's foreign policy: Selected; Sept. 1946 (New Delhi Publication Division,1961 Ministry of Information and Broadcasting, Govt. of India), p. 38.

17. South Asia was represented by delegation from Afghanistan, Bhutan, Srilanka, India and Nepal.

18. Keesing's Contemporary Archives, 1947, p. 8862.

19. William Henderson, The Development of Regionalism in South East Asia, International Organization, Vol.9, No. 4, November 1955, p. 476.

20. Report of the first Asian Relations Conference, New Delhi, ICWA, 1948.

21. Keesing's Contemporary Archives, 1947, p. 8862.

22. Jawaharlal Nehru's speeches, 1946-1949, p. 327.

23. Quoted by Harris Wofford, An American Interpretation of India's Asia policy, India's Role in Asia, p. 131.

24. N. Prasad, The Colombo Plan, India Quarterly, April— June, 1952, p 15.
25. Harris Walford, no. 15, p. 146.
26. Including delegations from South Asian countries - Afghanistan, India, Nepal, Pakistan, Srilanka.
27. Facts on File, 18-24, 1956.
28. New York Times, 20 July 1956.
29. Economic Weekly, 14 October 1961.
30. Lait Prasad Singh, The Politics of Economic Co-operation in Asia (Colombo University Press, 1966), pp. 3-12.
31. W.W. Rostow, The United States and the Regional Organization of Asia and the Pacific, 1965-1985 (Austin Texas; University of Texas Press, 1986), p. 131. See also Norman D. Palmer, op.cit., p. 78.
32. Nancy Jetly, Emergence of SAARC, in Bimal Prasad (ed.), Regional Co-operation in South. Asia; Problems and Prospects, (New Delhi; Vikas Publishing House 1989), P. 62.
33. S.D. Muni and Anuradha Muni, op. cit., p. 30.
34. Ceylon Daily News, 18 April 1981.
35. S.D. Muni and Anuradha Muni, n. 10, p. 35.
36. The Hindustan Times (New Delhi), 10 December, 1985.
37. 10 December, 1985.
38. The Tribune, 10 December 1985.
39. Dawn (Karachi), 11 December 1985.
40. 12 December 1985.
41. 12 December 1985
42. 10 December 1985.
43. 14 December 1985.
44. Hindustan Times (New Delhi) 7 December 1985.
45. Times of India (New Delhi), 8 December 1985

# 3

# Aims and Objectives of SAARC

The birth of SAARC was preceded by prolonged deliberations among the South Asian States which ultimately resulted into the signing of the Dhaka Declaration of 1985. In this declaration, the desire of the people of this region for greater co-operation, their mutual respect, equality, shared benefits etc figured prominently. Dhaka Declaration, which obscures for more than it reveals, 'incorporates very little that is concrete in terms of regional co-operation in the political, economic, cultural, technical and information spheres and offers very broad, often fundamental formulation that leave themselves open to a variety of interpretation in each country'[1].

Bangladesh prepared and circulated the draft paper in November 1980. It had three important features. First of all, the objectives of regional co-operation were defined in very wide terms. The scope of co-operation was not viewed as confined narrowly to economic matters, but as 'promoting active co-operation among countries of the region on matters of common interest in the economic, social, cultural, technical and Scientific, as well as in such other fields as may be agreed upon.... "Wider scope was envisaged not only in the areas of co-operation, but also in terms of geographical extent because one of the objectives identified in the draft was to "explore all avenues of closer co-operation between the countries of South Asia and the other Regional and International Organizations with similar aims and objectives".

The founding fathers were in favour of keeping the activities of the SAARC limited at a modest level in the sphere of co-operation off among themselves in the of peripheral importance[2], mainly in non-political sphere. But in this age of primacy of politics it is perhaps imparitical to expect that such a non-political approach would yield success. The founding fathers were afraid that raising politics would generate diverse currents which would run counter to the organization and hence decided that 'let there be taboo on politics now'[3]. However, they had to admit that it would not be possible to avoid politics too long. King Jigme Wangchuk of Bhutan had aptly remarked that it might neither be possible nor desirable to limit SAARC discussions to issue of a non-political nature, for the political climate of the region would certainly cast a long shadow over the deliberations.

Bilateral and contentious issues have been kept outside the purview of the deliberations of the SAARC (Art. 10(20)). The major reason behind such a provision was the Indian fear of being ganged up by her smaller neighbours with most of whom she has bilateral problems. It would provide them a platform to unite against her. At the Dhaka Summit (1985) Prime Minister Rajiv Gandhi apprehended that if bilateral issues were allowed in SAARC deliberation, they would generate stresses and strains impinging on regional co-operation and ultimately jeopardy-sing its very existence. Human psychology precludes the possibility of overlooking bilateral bitterness and rendering ungrudging co-operation at the regional or multilateral level. The basis of regional co-operation would be strengthend if a workable understanding could be forged among the countries concerned at the bilateral level[4].

Of course, it can be argued that pending the creation of

warm bilateral relations it is better to give the possibility of regional co-operation a fair trial. This half a loaf is obviously better than no bread at all. But it cannot be denied that by keeping the bilateral contentious issues alive one cannot except much from the SAARC. In fact, it would be too simplistic to wish away the lack of mutual trust and the existence of problems that vitiates the relations of the countries of the region at the bilateral level and to reanimate them in the process of regional co-operation.

The sovereign equality has been one of the guiding principles of the SAARC [Art. 2(1)], political reality has bestowed special importance upon India and Pakistan. They are the two principal states whose interactions, perception and images have a real bearing on the emerging pattern of relationship among the countries of the region[5]. Thus much of the prospect of the success of the SAARC is contingent upon the development of a cordial, at least not a hostile, relationship between the two regional super powers. But they are locked in a relationship of perpetual animosity. Mutual suspicion, mistrust and acrimony have become almost an obsession with both of them. It has cast a dark shadow not only upon their bilateral relations, but also upon the prospect of regional co-operation in South Asia[6].

## Major Objectives of the SAARC

The major objectives of the SAARC are very emphatically and clearly stated in the Dhaka Declaration adopted at the first SAARC Summit as will appear from the following exerpts:

"The Heads of State or Government reaffirmed that their fundamental goal was to accelerate the process of economic and social development in their respective countries through the optimum utilization of their human and material sources, so as to promote the welfare and prosperity of their peoples and to improve their quality of life. They were conscious that peace and security essential prerequisites for the realization of this objectives".

"The Heads of State or Government acknowledged that the countries of South Asia, who constituted one-fifth of humanity were faced with the formidable challenges posed by poverty, under development, low level of production, unemployment and pressure of population compounded by exploitation of the past and other adverse legacies. They felt that, bound as their countries were by many common values rooted in their social, ethnic, cultural and historical traditions, regional co-operation provided a logical response to these problems. They were conscious of their individual and regional strengths, their potential as a huge market, their substantial human and natural resources and the complement arities of their economies. They were confident that with effective regional co-operation, they could make optimum use of these capacities for the benefit of their people, accelerate the pace of their economic development and enhance their national and collective self-reliance. They were convinced that their countries, which had made important contributions to the enrichment of human civilization could together play their due role in International Relations and influence decisions which affected them".

At the most fundamental level, the regional goals should address the following :

(i) Problems of Poverty, hunger, unemployment, disease, illiteracy, which are shared by all the Member Countries of the SAARC;

(ii) acceleration of social and economic development with a view to improving the quality of life of the region;

(iii) achievement of collective self-reliance, with due regard to the national aspiration of the Member countries;

(iv) enhancement of the region's role in the global context;

(v) building regional structures to serve as a basis for reducing conflict producing tensions and promoting amity and understanding.

Though the goals of regional co-operation adopted by

the SAARC embrace specially selected areas of economic and cultural activities, there is a clear awareness of the mutually supporting roles of such co-operation in the political field. As a matter of fact, one of the important objectives that inspired the countries of the region to participate in the SAARC was to create, through regional co-operation in economic and cultural fields, an environment, conductive to confidence building and generation of friendly and constructive co-operation in the political field.

It is obvious that the South Asian leaders participating in the Dhaka Summit of the SAARC forcefully stated that the common threats facing all the countries in the region were embeded in the problems of poverty and under-development which were vastly aggravated by the deteriorating world economic situation.

The SAARC reflects the social and political realities of the region and seeks unity in diversity. The SAARC is not a new bloc or alliance based on shared perception of external threats. It cannot be overstressed that the proneness to borrow paradigms from entirely different social and political context may be as abortive as empirical generalizations from experiences of successful or unsuccessful regional co-operation in socially and politically different situations can be misleading. As a matter of fact, SAARC does not include any matter of regional security (against external affairs). Besides, the SAARC creates a new and complementary set of relations without intruding on the existing bilateral and multilateral relations of the Member-States. Another important element in the concept of the SAARC as a confidence - building measure is that it is not to be viewed as a supra-national organization. On state alone or in combination can impose a decision because unanimity and not consensus is the basis of all decisions. The sovereign equality of all Member States in the decision-making process is, thus, fully assured[7].

The objectives of the South Asian Regional co-operation

had been couched in broad based terms, and appropriate to the occasion. These had been addressed to the needs of better life both at individual and collective levels. These objectives are:

(a) to promote the welfare of the peoples of South Asia and to improve the quality of life;

(b) to accelerate economic growth, social progress and cultural development in the region;

(c) to promote and strengthen collective self-reliance among the countries of South Asia;

(d) to contribute to mutual trust, understanding and appreciation of one another's problems;

(e) to promote active collaboration and mutual assistance in the economic, social, cultural, technical and scientific fields;

(f) to strengthen co-operation with other developing countries ;

(g) to strengthen co-operation among themselves, in Inter-national forums on matters of common interest;

(h) to co-operate with International Regional organization with similar aims and purposes.

In view of the socio-political milieu of division and diversity, it was perhaps prudent that the founders decided to exclude political issues from the agenda of SAARC in order to safeguard the organisation from being destroyed by political controversy in the early stage of its evolution. However, recent events in South Asia and their impact on SAARC compel one to raise the fundamental issues[8].

At the first Summit itself, the late President of Pakistan, Zia-Ul-Haque raised the contentious Kashmir issue as "a stumbling block" to regional co-operation in South Asia. The former Srilankan President Jayawardene was also quite unhappy about India's alleged intervention in the civil war of Srilanka as a result of terrorism by the Tamil rebels in the North Eastern and in the North regions. At the second

Summit held in Bangalore during November 1996, the mutual bicherings among these nation-states surfaced again. For instance, the Pak Representative, Mohammad Khan Junejo with an obvious hint cowards India emphasized in his inaugural speech that the SAARC member countries should notify one another about significant troop movement and thereby help in confidence - building measures. King Birendra of Nepal emphasized the psyche of his government about the need for genuine respect for sovereign equality of the nations and the need of "give and take". On the other hand, all other South Asian leaders took a positive stand at Bangalore to further broaden the areas of regional co-operation, so as to include some activities for wider people-to-people participation[9].

The SAARC objectives are not confined to economic co-operation alone. They also focus on promoting and strengthening "collective self-reliance and contributing to mutual trust, understanding and appreciation of one another problem" among the countries of the region. It implies that the broad objectives of the SAARC does not preclude co-operation in the politico-strategic field at a later stage. The present scope of co-operation although limited should pave the way for broader understanding and consequently co-operation in expanded fields at a future time. In fact the emergence of an unified stand on some of the international issues is a major pre-requisite for evolving a comprehensive regional programme for co-operation.

The SAARC has provided the vital mechanism. The hectic SAARC process provided numerous occasions for wide interaction for both officials and academics. As this interaction goes on there is enough scope of building confidence, averting crisis and creating congenial environ for co-operation. Some positive signs can be seen from the fact that degree and level of interaction between academics of various countries has substantially increased. That the academics of regional states have been able to meet and discuss various facts of our problems including sensitive security Matters is an indication of breaking the barriers - at least psychological. Informally, the SAARC meetings have provided occasions for the member countries to sort out bilateral political matters. The Indo-Pak foreign Minister's dialogue that continued from Pakistan to Male in July 1984 even abroad the aircraft is a typical example. There are small but significant steps towards the resolution of contentious bilateral issues. And SAARC without getting directly involved is facilitating such steps. SAARC has the potential to cast its long shadow on the contentious bilateral issues of the region even without getting involved in them. If this potential groups SAARC may acquire a politico-strategic dimension while continuing its forge and consolidated infrastructural and co-operative linkage in various functional areas[10].

A major objectives of various regional groupings, irrespective of whether these have formal or informal trading arrangements, is to increase intraregional trade and at the sometime also appropriate a large share of the gains arising out of expansion of world trade. Recently all the SAARC countries have carried out major reforms in their economic policies with a view to meet the new challenges emerging out of increasing globalization. These reforms which are intended to enable to SAARC countries to integrate themselves with the global economy, can also help them to achieve economic co-operation among themselves. The reforms have provided a new set of opportunities for the private sector in these countries for forging closer industrial and commercial relations.

While trade liberalisation and expansion within the region are important, joint action to promote investment and stimulate agricultural and industrial production is necessary to exploit the full potential of regional co-operation. The strategy should serve to exploit the region's complementarities in natural resources, technology, finance, managerial talent and market. There is a vast scope for involving the business sectors, both public and private, in joint undertakings. There are well established private sector companies in the SAARC region possessing financial, technological and managerial capabilities. There are important assets that provide new avenues for joint production arrangements in many areas.

The expansion of infrastructural facilities such as banking, insurance, telecommunications and transport is vital for industrial development. Some of the SAARC countries, many not be able to make significant progress on their own in expanding infrastructural facilities. Regional economic co-operation can make an important contribution in this field. There is also a crucial need for implementing supportive policies in areas such as legal framework and payments arrangements. Many SAARC countries cannot be self-sufficient in educational facilities at higher levels like scientific, technical and professional fields. The dependence on the higher levels like scientific, technical and professional fields. The dependence on the higher educational institutions in the industrial countries can be reduced by making wider use of the scientific, technical and management institutions already established in some of the SAARC countries. Technical and vocational training could be expanded through technical assistance programmes within the region.

The SAARC countries can co-operate with each other in undertaking joint efforts to protect the environment in the several areas in managing shared natural resources, especially river basins, coastal areas, forests and wildlife, in activities like in-share and off-share oil exploration, the management of exclusive economic zones and the prevention of desertification, and in many other frontier areas of research as such as biotechnology, reneuable sources, energy, especially biomass, wind and solar energy and the efficient use of energy in agriculture, industry, transport and households.

Primary commodities continue to be an important source of foreign exchange earnings for some of the SAARC countries. The sharp fluctuation in commodity prices pose a continuous threat to these countries. Attempts to achieve producer/consumer co-operation in securing stable markets for commodities have not been quite successful, while competition among producers in adversely affected the interests of all the producer countries. Since the SAARC countries account for a substantial share in the world markets for some primary commodities, increased regional co-operation could help in obtaining remunerative and stable prices through supply management or market intervention. This co-operation should also extend to consultations among SAARC countries with a view to taking common positions in negotiations in International commodity markets and in dealing with the consumer countries.

Expansion of intra-regional trade in the SAARC region can be facilitated through supportive policies such as removal of trade restrictions, widening the range of products covered by tariff/trade preferences and provision of deeper reduction of tariffs. Trade expansion can also be facilitated by the regional co-ordination of investments in selected fields. Opportunities are efficient import substitution within the region have to be identified and pursued by the private sector.

There are various technical requirements concerning the implementation of the Uruguay Round of Agreements. Many member countries of SAARC do not have the necessary resources to assess these requirements and adopt suitable measures for taking advantage of the new trading arrangements on the one hand and for avoiding the negative results arising from the Agreements. The SAARC countries can co-operate among themselves in this area with a view to maximize the gains out of the new multilateral training arrangement.[11]

## Possible Areas of Co-operation

President Zia-Ur-Rahman in his letter addressed to the Heads of Government of the region briefly touched on the underlying factors which prompted him to take the initiative. He mentioned that while other regions had evolved institutional arrangements for consultations on matters of mutual interest and co-operation in the economic, social and cultural fields on the regional basis, and had consequently benefited immensely from such co-operation, the only region which did not have any such arrangements for regional co-operation was the South Asian region which comprised one-fifth of the world population.

Bangladesh President in his letter tentatively indicated economic, technical, scientific, social and cultural fields as possible areas for regional co-operation. Such co-operation is not, however, intended to take the form of any new block or alliance. The Institutional Arrangements set up for such co-operation would strictly conform to the principle of non-alingment to which all the countries in the region are firmly committed.

Any proposal for economic co-operation must consequently be formulated with the greatest care in order to ensure that the weak are not exploited and that the strong do not dominated. The areas selected should only be those in which co-operation will mutually benefit all the countries irrespective to existing economic disparties, so as to make regional co-operation meaningful, strengthen the spirit of mutual trust and understanding and bridge the development gaps existing among the countries of the region.

A final argument in favour of such co-operation is that it is only through regional cohesion that South Asia can hope to have an effective voice in International Forums. The countries of South Asia share many common values that are rooted in their social, ethnic, cultural and historical traditions. Perception about certain specific events or political situation of the world may differ, but such differences do not seem to create a gap between them that cannot be bridged.

Regional co-operation in South Asia as elsewhere in the world should in no way, intrude on the existing bilateral and multilateral relations of the countries of the region, nor does the proposal envisage either the substitution or the disruption of existing co-operation between or amongst the countries of the region in other Forums. In SAARC, the co-operation in the economic sphere could be the starting point which could be expanded to include social and cultural co-operation. Science and technology also seem to offer great possibilities. Within these very broad parameters one can identify certain fields in which co-operation will not only be highly beneficial, but also present a maximum convergence of common interest. In selecting these fields one will have to bear in mind the need to avoid duplication and overlapping functions and jurisdictions. Based on the clearly identified needs in various sectors of our economy as well as the common developmental objectives facing the countries of this region, it is felt that the following areas are the most suitable for co-operation :

(a) **Tele-Communication** - Tele-communication happens to be an integral part of the economic infrastructure in every society. Economic activities, dissemination of knowledge vastly expanded social contacts of highly mobile individuals in contemporary societies, and last but not the least, trade and commerce, depend upon an efficient tele-communication network. A tele-communication system in a country can attain its optimum level of efficiency and usefulness, if it can be linked up with similar systems in neighbouring countries. As at present, it is a fact that in South Asia, it is easier to communicate with Europe and America than with next door neighbour.

(b) **Meteorology** - In the field of meterology, co-operation could pay rich dividents to the member countries of the South Asia region. Facilities for scientific weather forecasting and introduction of the latest techniques of and methods for the study of climatic patterns could be organized on a regional basis, Since, most of the countries of the region face permanent exposure to the hazards of cyclonic storms and other such natural disasters, active co-operation towards sharing the fund of knowledge, techniques, data etc. gathered in this area will be significantly benefited to the member countries. These efforts would naturally be designed to strengthen the present International Arrangements that may co-operative in the region.

Countries of South Asian Region are first establish adequate national information systems and through consuitation and co-operation plan on a South Asian Regional Information System for Science and technology, It is obvious that the emphasis on the data which will be available in the Regional Information System would primarily be based on the areas of sectors which are of common interest to the countries of the South Asian Region. In this context, the existing Regional Centre for Transfer of Technology - get-up at Bangalore under the auspicious of ESCAP could be profitably used by the countries from the South Asian Region.

(c) **Transport** - In order to ensure an effective flow of movement of goods and also to facilitate intra-regional trafic, a well-integrated system of communications especially in the form of road and railways links, would be invaluable for economic development of the region. The national plans for building roads and for establishing railways lies could be harmonised at the frontiers to allow easy access across the national borders without any substantial additional cast. Co-operation in this area would bring the countries closer through increased surface mobility.

(d) **Shipping** - The importance of shipping in the external trade of any country, whether costal or land-locked, can hardly be over-emphasized. Its relative advantage well- recognised.

The world shipping market at present is overwhelming dominated by the developed countries. Thus, conditions imposed by these countries and the liner conference arrangements controlled by them militate against the natural desire of developing countries to increase their tonnage capacity for a greater share in the transportation of sea cargo. The frequent escalation in the freight charges adversely affect the development needs and the balance of payments position of developing countries. The countries in South Asian region suffer from the consequent disadvantages in varying degrees. Thus in order to bring about a degree of self-sufficiency in this field and to give an additional fillip to economic development of countries of this region. Shipping is a natural area for co-operation on a regional basis.

(e) **Tourism** - Tourism is another area where there co-operation exists a vast potential for intra-regional co-operation. The revolutionary growth of air transportationin recent times has made tourism the second largest export industry in the world. It is essential that South Asia/ gets a greater share o the world market.

The potential of the region to attract tourism is virtually unlimited. The combind efforts of the countries of the region can be geared to develop this potential to their common benefit. This can be done by strengthening the infra-structure at home and by a vigorous marketing effort abroad. The rich and ancient heritage of the sub-continent and the varied scenic beauty of different parts of the region will provide the necessary attraction for foreign visitors. Intra-regional tourism can also be a major force in forging greater understanding between and among the countries and peoples of the region.

The combined resources of South Asia can be tapped, better facilities can be provided to tourist which would doubtless increase their number. For instance, joint package, tours with reduced group fares could be organised their could be co-operation among the various travel agencies operating in the region that could enable co-ordinated - tour programmes, common tourist policies could be evolved after due consultations among the concerned government.

(f) **Agricultural Research** - The Agricultural sector has been identified as the most important one for the countries of the South Asian Region. There is a need for increasing Agricultural productivity is almost all these countries. The various methods of Irrigation have to be optimized and improvement brought about appropriate inputs in science and technology. It is obvious that collaborative efforts in the area of Agricultural Research could be beneficial to almost all the countries in South Asian Region.

South Asian countries given their dependence on this sector already have a large number of institutions engaged in research and development in a wide variety of fields. Regional co-operation would usefully augment the growing fund of knowledge and techniques in these fields. A co-ordinated Arrangement for sharing information, experiences and results of experiments, etc., could effectively hasten the process of growth and productivity in this vital sector. Similarly, in view of the importance of developing the rural sector in particular, exchange of ideas and sharing of experience in the sphere of rural institution-building could resuslt in significant advances as well as saving both in resources and time.

(g) **Rural Development** - Science and majority of the population in the South Asian Region is dependent on Agricultural actively and is at the same time based in rural environment, it is necessary to identify developmental programmes in which science and technology could provide valuable input. This would involve proper understanding of the culture, social and conomic background of the rural population. In view of the commonalities of many of these factors in the countries of the region, it is felt that the process of application of science and technology for Rural Development can be jointly studied by groups of countries from this region. This is an area where scientists from the developed countries would not be able to understand our problems; and their conclusions are unlikely to be applicable to our problems, more importantly, the efforts in this area have to be entirely based on indigenous capabilities for which a co-operative approach in our region would definitely be helpful.

(h) **Joint Ventures** - An economic co-operation group creates a wider market for commodities requiring large scale production. It also provides a scope utilisation of hither to unexploited resources through more efficient organization and optimum employment of existing resources. By increasing the range of production and ensuring higher returns on capital, it can create a self-sustained basis for further; co-operation. Such multilateral economic groups not only can attract capital and technology form outside, but also obtain exemptions from GATT rules on non-discriminatory treatment on trade. Joint ventures provide the most potent field for reaping all these advantages for countries belonging to such a group. It is also one of the most tangible and productive forms of co-operation within the framework of ECDC.

The countries in South Asian Region passess a wide range of natural and mineral resources, technical know-how, trained manpower and a vast market. It spite of the fact that these countries are at varying stages of development, it is possible to identify potential areas for Joint Ventures, evolve appropriate industrial framework and policy instruments on the basis of equitable benefit occurring to these countries. Co-operative endevaours in the economic field can be undertaken to expand the product base through joint ventures that will lead to the creation of other favourable factors for further co-operation.

(g) **Market Promotion: Selected Commodities** - The countries of South Asia enjoy a significant share of the world market for a number of commodities, such as tea, jute and cotton.

Most of these countries have separately undertaken marketing and promotional efforts for these commodities. It is well recognised that joint initiatives can reduce promotional cast and have greater impact on the export markets. Moreover, this will also enable the countries of South Asia, particularly the less developed among them, to take full advantage of the liberal measures available under the generalised system of preferences (GSP) in the market of the developed countries. In the face of growing competion from substitutes as well as uncertainties due to price fluctuations, such joint initiatives will provide additional guarantee for further expansion of markets at remunerative prices.

(j) **Scientific and Technological Co-operation** – Countries of the South Asian region have a special need to develop effective use of science and technology for alleviating the widespread poverty that is a common characteristic of the area. It is recognised that the promotion of scientific education will not achieve the desired results unless science can be applied in practical terms for the development of agriculture, industry, energy and all other needs of society. There is needed ample scope for further programmes in the field of applied science and technology to meet the basic requirements of the people of the region, particularly those in the rural areas. In many cases, the experiences gained by these countries in this sphere can be shared with greater advantage than technology borrowed from the industrialised countries of the developed world.

Co-operation in this field is particularly relevant in regard to both conventional and non-conventional sources of energy. Such co-operation could explore ways and means of reducing dependence on Foreign Resources by the development of local energy sources, improvement of efficient energy use through development of low energy technology; conservation of non-renewable energy resources, etc.

Concerned research and action-oriented programmes for eradiction and elimination of such diseases as malaria, cholera etc. afflicting the people of this region could also be an effective and useful area of co-operation.

(k) **Use of Sophisticated Technologies** - The developed countries often project a concept that for poor developing countries what is needed are simple technologies and not the sophisticated technologies which are more relevant to their society. This concept has to be challenged in attempting to solve the problems of the developing society. As a specific example, one would like to quote the possibility of using a sophisticated Geo-synchronous Satellite for the purpose of education a massive scale through use of Satellite, television broadcasting; for proving telecommunication linkages between rural and remote areas for studying global weather pattern where it is relevant to the particular region of developing countries and subsequently devising improvement for weather forecasting and possible modification, etc. Satellite technology could also be used for the major task of carrying out resources survey through the technique of remote sensing. Basic training in many of these areas could have a fruitful spin-off in the overall growth of the countries sophisticated areas of science and technology. Such as electronics, computer sciences, telecommunication, remote sensing are some of the areas which are well within the capabilities and reach of scientists and engineers from the South Asian region, if a proper infrastructure involving training, is built up Collaborative projects between our region could enhance the capabilities of individual countries and the application of sophisticated technologies on a collaborative basis could be very useful. As a possible idea, one could consider the use of a single Geo-synchronous Satellite by the countries of the South Asian Region for the purpose of satellite TV, metereology etc. The burden of high costs and the related import of equipment could be considerably reduced if the countries of the region agree to work on a collaborative basis in acquiring such a Satellite system for their region.

These are some of the areas which appear to be extremely beneficial for carrying out collaborative programmes in science and technology in the South Asian region. There are a number of other areas which have to be eventually identified after they have had a through understanding and knowledge about each other's capabilities and interests in Science and technology.

(1) **Educational and Technical Co-operation** - Co-operation at International and Regional level with regard to education has now been well established and institutionalised in many regions. In this region also, shared experiences of the countries could be usefully exchanged in matters pertaining to this subject.

A primary common concern among these countries is,

for instance, how to provide cast-effective educational services which could reach out to millions of school age children who crowd the cities and villages. The experiences of countries of the region, ranging from such areas as book production, manufacture of low cast scientific equipment to matters connected with curriculum formation, examination procedures, teacher's training and in-service training, nonformal education, just to name a few, could be usefully shared.

These countries having similar problems could benefit more from the expertise of personnel in the region than from that of foreign experts who obtain their training in an entirely different environment, and who, consequently fail to develop to correct orientation in dealing with regional problems. Workshops, seminars, conferences and visit of technical experts organized on a regional basis could provide useful exchange of knowledge and experience.

(m) **Cultural Co-operation** - The South Asian countries are heirs to some of the richest cultural tradition of the world. The influence of the major religions - Hinduism, Buddhism, Christianity and Islam - on the different countries of the region in varying degrees, has contributed to the richness and diversity in the cultural heritage of these countries. This is, therefore, a field in which regional co-operation can be of considerable benefit in a better understanding of the cultural heritage of the countries in the region and, as a result, in promoting mutual goodwill. As a matter of fact, cultural exchanges are already taking place between these countries on the basis of bilateral agreements. A regional approach would, however, introduce a new dimension in the cultural exchange programmes.

One can readily see numerous possibilities. There can be, for example, a South Asian Regional Film Festival in one of the capitals. Also exhibitions of paintings can be organised on a regional basis. These can become a major source of encouragement for artistic activities within the region. Handicrafts of the different countries of the region can also be enriched by holding exhibitions on a regional basis from time to time. Sports is another field which offers great possibilities. South Asian Games and Sports organised on an annual basis can become an integral part of the cultural life of the area. All these possibilities clearly indicate that the cultural field in a area that has a very wide scope for co-operationin the South Asian Region[12].

The Integrated Programme of Action (IPA), which covers the activities in the above mentioned area, has so far resulted in over six-hundred activities mainly in the form of workshops and seminars, but also including preparation of state of the Art Reports on some subjects, meetings of Scientists, etc. All this ammounts to exchange of experiences and does not go beyond that to the formulation of regional programmes of research or result in any transfer of technology. Even the regional centres in the field of agriculture, tuberculosis, and documentation, work in a peripheral manner. Nevertheless, it can be maintained that, in spite of all constraints and lacunae, functional co-operation in the framework of SAARC its value, and its utility has been acknowledged and acclaimed. Even if such co-operation is constantly be set by the issue of relative gains, one way of overcoming the fear of unequal exchange is to recognise its certain transcendent integrative value. Functional co-operation is an asset for finding rational solutions to shared problems. But its success has value if areas of functional co-operation are not chosen at random but carefully selected for possible spill over effects into areas with greater political and economic salience.

Diverse objectives guided the member countries of SAARC to join and participate in Regional Organisation. In the case of Bangladesh, the principal mover of SAARC, personal aspirations of President, Zia-Ur-Rahman, and seeking legitimacy of his popular regime by playing an important International role provided a strong impetus. Bangladesh was strongly supported in this venture by small countries like Nepal, Bhutan, Srilanka and Maldives. Generally, it suits the interests of all smaller neighbours of India to use regional forum to bargain collectively with India for securing concessions on various economic issues affecting each of them bilateral. They achieved considerable success in this regard.

Pakistan, unlike the smaller members, was cautious initially. However, fearing isolation it did not find to prudent to resist the move beyond a point. While working to thwart India's presence and influence, it tried to improve its equastions with other SAARC members. As a result, Pakistan significantly improved its understanding with Bhutan, Nepal and Srilanka.

India pursued two prolonged strategy to advance its regional objectives through SAARC. One was to expand and consolidate infrastructural and social linkages at various levels among these countries and create a basis for interdependence. Secondly, it tried to evolve consensus in SAARC on International economic and political issues in order to strengthen its bargaining position in North-South and other sensitive political issues debated in the UN or other International Forums[13].

It is often emphasised that SAARC is not a political organisation, but an organization for economic co-operation. Besides, the IPA focusing only on economic and technical issues, the SAARC charter, under Article X general provisions, categorically stipulates that:

(i) decision at all levels shall be taken by unanimity and,

(ii) bilateral and contentious issues shall be excluded from the deliberations.

In view of the socio-political milieu of division and diversity, it was perhaps prudent that the founders decided to exciude political issues from the agenda of SAARC in order to safeguard the organization from being destroyed by political controversy in the early state of its evolution. However, recent events in South Asia and their impact on SAARC compel one to raise the fundamental issues[14].

## Various Issues

When the SAARC was born, the high expectations among the common people that it would start a new era of co-operation and goodwill in the region. In the Dhaka Declaration, the desire of the people of this region for greater co-operation, their mutual respect, equality, shared benefits etc. figured prominently. But these homilies could not compensate for the lacunae in the fields of articulation and concretization of the objectives of the SAARC. It has been pointed out by a scholar that the Dhaka Declaration, which obscures for more that it reveals, incorporates very little that is concrete in terms of regional co-operation in the political, economic, cultural, technical and information spheres and offers very broad, often fundamental formulations that leave themselves open to a variety of interpretations in each country[15].

Bilateral and contentious issues have been kept outside the purview of the deliberations of the SAARC [Art. 10(2)]. The major reason behind such a provision was the Indian fear of being ganged up by her smaller neighbours with most of whom she has bilateral problems. At the Dhaka Summit (1985) Prime Minister Rajiv Gandhi apprehended that if bilateral issues were allowed in SAARC deliberation they would generate strosses and strains impinging on regional co-operation and ultimately jeopardi-sing its very existence.

The self-perception of the South Asian Countries and their inclination towards pursuing course of action without regard to the common interest of the region and their poor track record to act as partner of co-operation have also prevented them from building up an identity of outlook towards International Issues - both economic and political. They perceive the global situation so differently that it is difficult to evolve a common strategy and attempt a collective regional response even to vital global issues[16]. All the SAARC countries are members of the non-alignment. But in the case of smaller and Regional Organizations greater cohesion among the members of greater identity of outlook are the normal expectation. In the case of the SAARC, however the member states not only do not belong to the same wave length so far as International Issues are concerned but they also look at things at the International level from different and even conflicting angles. History of International Relations are so repete with such instances that it hardly warrants further elaboration. The velocity of contrigugal forces operating in this region may also be guaged from the fact that even a prominent member of the region, Pakistan, likes to search her identity more as a West Asian rather than as a South Asian State.

Though, sovereign equality has been one of the guiding principles of the SAARC [Art. 2(1)]. Political reality has bestowed special importance upon India and Pakistan. They are the two principal states whose inter-actions, perception and images have a real bearing on the emerging pattern of relations among the countries of the region[17]. Thus much of the prospect of the success of the SAARC is contigent upon the development of a cardial, at least not a hostile, relationship between the two regional super powers. But they are locked in a relationship of perpetual animosity. Mutual suspicion, misturst and acrimony have become almost an obsession with both of them. It has cast a dark shadow not only upon their bilateral relations but also upon the prospect of regional co-operation in South Asia.

Collective economic benefit has been the main rationale as well as drive behind SAARC, but even economic co-operation is dictated so heavily by political constraints that it looked pretty hard to exploit the regions potential.

The South Asian region has been an interplay of the politics of no war and no peace syndrome politics of conflict dominates at present. The centre piece of South Asia's political system is the Indo-Pakistan relationship, in the absence of a satisfactory resolution of conflicts between the two states mutual distrust and hostility will continue to simmer even after the SAARC formation. It may be more pragmatic to assume that in South Asia the resolution of conflicts will result in the economic and political success of the SAARC. SAARC, at best, can lead the two to table but cannot make them talk for resolution of their conflict.

Intensification of the Arms race in the sub-continent between India and Pakistan since 1971 is another irritant and may mar the future prospects of SAARC. Both India and Pakistan, if they realise that a peaceful and stable South Asia will free their energies so that they can play positive and major roles Regionally and Internationally, that itself will be a major achievement for SAARC.

Another issues is Nepal's Water Resources. Allocation of Ganges Water Farraka in Bangladesh between India and Bangladesh remain's a sore point. With the formation of SAARC it is assumed that an amicable answer could be found out more easily in a region framework, treating this as an economic rather than a political problem.

In certain regional organizations, like EEC, politics may play a negligible role in the economic decisions of the organizations, but not so far South Asia where politics will dictate the degree of economic co-operation so that the prospects of the latter is tied to the progress of the former. Speech of King Jigme Wangchuck of Bhutan at the Summit is relevant in this regard. He expressed doubt and felt that it might neither be possible nor desirable to limit SAARC discussions to issue of a non-political nature, for the political climate of the region would certainly cast a long shadow over the deliberations. One can say that at least, SAARC has made a beginning towards economic, cultural and social co-operation in a limited manner among member States. SAARC priorties will be predo-minantly economic co-operation, the removal of artificial barriers to trade and avoidance of mutual competition in seeking markets outside the region. The mechanism provided, in principle, for consultations on problems specific to the region could prove useful at a later date provided serious economic and political content based on shared interests, values and objectives, can be developed gradually with the SAARC forum.

The Dhaka Declaration, obscures for more than it reveals about the state of the political art and of the reality of interstate relations in the South Asian region. It incorporate very little that is concrete in terms of regional co-operation in the political, economic, cultural, technical and information spheres and offers very broad, often fundamental formulations that leave themselves open to a variety of interpretations in each country, especially when one recalls that they issue jointly from the Governments of India, Pakistan, Srilanka, Bangladesh and so forth. At the consensual level their will be disappointments that India has not succeeded in placing the business of economic development - trade, industry, energy and so on - squarely within the scope of SAARC. In other worlds, the recognition that the South Asian region can be treated in a special way as an economic zone and that substantive developmental activity can be facilitated and perhaps co-ordinated activity on a regional basis is still being resisted - presumably under the misconceived apprehension that India as the biggest and most developed economic power in the region will be tempted to dominate the larger market. This is comparable, ofcourse, to the insinuations and hang-ups that are being expressed by some of the Regional Statesman flother critics concerning tendencies towards "hegemonisms" at the political level.

India's position was spelled out clearly by Prime Minister Rajeev Gandhi in his address to the Summits which stands as a guarantee for those who always cherish a negative attitude towards India. SAARC has materialised after painstaking efforts over the past some years. If the seven countries can add further dimensions to it, that is to be welcomed. As expected by other nations of the region it will only be served if India alone showed magnanimity. Other nations duly reciprocated for fruitful co-operation.

The unified and systematic efforts of the states in the South Asian region is giving a concrete shape to the idea of the SAARC have, by all accounts, already set a commendable example in regional co-operation. At the same time it would be idle to deny that misgivings about the future of the SAARC continue to linger in the minds of many, including some who wish the SAARC level.

The selected economic areas of cooperation in the case of the SAARC embrace such vitally important sectors as agriculture, rural development, telecommunication, transport, meteorology, science and technology. Regional co-operation in these areas offers immense possibilities for concerted action in addressing some of the major problems of the region. The most formidable and fundamental among them is the problem of poverty, shared by all the countries in the region including India.

The problems of disparate development and lack of economic complementarity are placed in perspective when viewed in the context of their root causes, namely,

(i) the changes in the structure of economy inherited from the colonial era and the continuing structural dependence of the countries in the region on the industrial economies; and

(ii) prevailing inequitable World Economic Order rendering closer co-operation among developing countries impera-tive with a view to reforming this order. The continuing structural dependence of the countries in the region on the industrial economies has resulted in the loss of a large proportion of their surplus to the industrial countries due to unfavourable trade mechanism and terms, repatriation of profits of Foreign Investors, and import of monopoly-period technology.(often outdated). The dependent industrial

> and economic growth has been further constrained by the fact that, though in theory the industrialized capitalist countries are committed to the market economy, the free operation of the market forces has been blocked by tariff and non-tariff barriers. Currently, the decline in the price of commodities is costing the developing countries as estimated amour of 65 billion annually.

The domestic policies of the countries of the region bearing on the planning strategy and the structure of production, employment and consumption are essentially similar. Regardless of differences in ideology and political and social structure, all countries in the region opted for 'mixed economy' and even where the society was characterized by plurality, the power structure remained elitist in character. Apprently inspired by the goal of rapid development and the example of the spectacular progress of the industrial countries, the planners and policy makers of South Asia borrowed concepts, models and strategies of development from these countries. Development was, for all practical intents and purposes, equated with economic growth with the focus on a modern, capital intensive industrial sector. Notwithstanding their good intentions and in some cases impressive growth rate, the overall result was a highly distorted growth pattern marked by mounting unemployment, increasing poverty and widening regional and rural-urban disparity. Burgeoning population and continuing conspicuous consumption by a few made the situation worse.

The problem of poverty poses a threat to the common security of the South Asian region. It clearly warrants concerted action on a regional basis since none of the states in isolation has been successful in finding an effective solution to this problem.

South Asian Regional co-operation encompasses Inter-Governmental co-operation in the framework of SAARC, as also co-operation in the wider process that involves Non-Governmental actors also.

## An Appraisal

Tremendous potentialities of Regional co-operation in South Asia exist both in economic and socio-cultural fields. In this context it cannot be overstressed that all of the nine selected areas of regional co-operation are of vital importance to the nation-building goals of the countries in the region. For example, agriculture still remains the largest single contributor to GDP and also the largest source of employment in the region taken as a whole. The development of agriculture to its full potential, besides generating more employment, could ensure food security for the region and thus be an important step in the direction of achieving the goal of collective self-reliance as envisaged in the SAARC Declaration. Both Agriculture and Rural Development have also a special significance as the poor live in the Rural Sector.

In addition to the already identified areas, vast possibilities for regional co-operation exist in some other very important fields. Trade is one of them. Bangladesh in its draft paper suggested co-operation in the field of 'Market Promotion' in selected commodities such as tea, Jute and Cotton. The existing level of intra-regional trade is very poor. It does not exceed, on an average, 5 to 6 percent this poor level of intra-regional trade by implication indicates the scope for expansion is considerable. All the South Asian neighbours suffer from adverse trade balance with India. The only exception in this respect is Pakistan which has possible balance of trade with India and that is mainly because Pakistan restricts its imports from India only to its public sector. The solution of this problem lies in India understanding to set up joint ventures in the neighbouring countries in those sectors where the concerned country has the abundance of raw materials.

In addition to the prospect of co-operation in trade and industrialization, South Asian countries can also profitably co-operate in developing and harnessing natural resources. The region has the abundance of hydropower and irrigation potential from its water-resources. A regional prospective on the sharing river waters may also take into account the question of judicious harnessing of the irrigation potential of these rivers.

Explotation of sea-bed resources of India, Srilanka, Bangladesh, Pakistan and Maldives is another area where wider co-operation in the region is possible and desirable. Not only hydro-power and oil, but energy as a whole may be an important field for regional co-operation. The scope for regional co-operation is no less promissing in the field of socio-cultural activities. A study group has been appointed for this with India as the co-ordinator and the first meeting of the group is likely to take place in Delhi by the end of June 1983.

The scope for regional interaction in the field of Education and Scientific Research is indeed very vast. Many possibilities for training in the field of science and technology may also be worked out. It such a trust and understanding is established greater harmony in strategic perspectives and security perceptions in South Asia will be facilitated[18].

SAARC is clearly a move in the right direction meeting the nation-building challenges, that face the states in the South Asian region. It is also in step with the new trends in the dynamics of International and Regional relations likely to act as catalytic forces leading to an equitable restructuring of the world political and economic order. The most heartening phenomenon in the contemporary world still shackled to outmoded and anti-democratic security concepts and structures is the rapidly expanding interdependence of the nations and growing extension and intensification of co-operation beneficial to peoples across the sovereign borders through International, Regional and Sub-Regional Associations of nation-states, The SAARC through building appropriate structures for mutually beneficial regional co-operation can strengthen this new trend and contribute significantly to the cause of peace, stability and progress Regionally and also Globally[19].

## References

1. V.K. Arora, 'SAARC : Prospects of Co-operation, India Quarterly, Vol. XLII, No. 1, January-March, 1986, p.72.
2. Muhammad Shamsul Hague, no. 2, p. 52.
3. President Zia-U1-Hague's remark to the journalists in Dhaka on 10 Dec. 1985, cited in Pran Chopra, 'The Rising Salience of Politics in SAARC', in Satish Kumar (ed.), Year Book on India's Foreign Policy 1984-85, 'Sage Publications, New Delhi, 1987, p. 99.
4. Amal Jayawardane, 'Finland Vs Srilanka: use and misuse of an Analogy' in S.U. Kgdikara (ed.), South Asian Strategic Issues : Srilankan Perspectives, Sage Publications, New Delhi, 1990, p. 131.
5. Lak Raj Baral; SAARC, But no SAARK : South Asian Regional co-operation in perspective; Pacific Affairs, Vol. 58, No. 3, Fall 1985, p. 418.
6. Bipattaram Ghosh, "SAARC : Some Major impediments to its success", Asian Studies, XIII (1), 1995; pp. 30-45.
7. M. Shamsul Haque, "South Asian Association for Regional co-operation, Past, present and future"; BIISS Journal, Vol. 7, No. 1, 1986, p. 424.
8. Shambhu R. Simkhada "Issues before the SAARC Summit", BIISS Journal Vol. 10, No. 4, 1989, pp. 419-420.
9. Mishra, P.K.; Dhaka to New Delhi : One decade of SAARC India Quarterly 52 (1-2), June 96, 73-86.
10. S.D. Muni, "Building Regionalism from Below", Asian Survey, Vol. XXV, No. 4, p. 404.
11. S.N. Raghavan, "Regional Economic Co-operation among SAARC Countries", pp. 1-10.
12. From SARC to SAARC: Milestones in the Evolution of Regional Co-operation in South Asia (1980-88), Vol.l, pp. 1-10.
13. Jagdish Lal, 'Historical Background of establishment of SAARC', Third Concept': An International Journal of Ideas;

Dec. 1993, Dp. 24.

14. Shambhu R. Simkhada, "Issues before the SAARC Summit"; BIISS Journal, Vol. 10, 1989, pp- 419-420.
15. V.K. Arora, "SAARC: Prospects of Co-operation"; India Quarterly, Vol. XLII, No. 1, January-March 1986, p. 72.
16. Jai Prakash Sharma, "SAARC : Problems and Prospects", Political Science Review, Vol. 26, Nos. 3-4, July-December, 1986.
17. Lok Raj Baral, 'SAARC, But no SAARK', South Asian Regional co-operation in perspective', Pacific Affairs, Vol. 58, No. 3, Fall, 1985, p. 418.
18. S.D. Muni & Anuradha Muni, 'Regional Co-operation in South Asia', (National Publishing House, New Delhi), pp. 44-65.
19. M. Shamsul Huque, "South Asian Association for Regional co-operation : Past, present and future", BISS Journal, Vol. 7, N. 1, 1986; p. 424.

# 4

# Structure and Functions of SAARC

The structure of SAARC is based largely on the ASEAN Model, though there are some important differences. Its Summits meet annually, barring in exceptional cases. The Summits are preceded by the preparatory meetings of the Council of Foreign Ministers and of the Standing Committee at the level of Council of Foreign Ministers and of the Standing Committee at the level of Foreign Secretaries. There is a committee now of economic co-operation too, at the level of Secretaries to the Government. There are nearly, a dozen of technical committee covering developmental areas from agriculture to Meteorology. The organization has its headquarters at Kathmandu headed by a Secretary General appointed for two years on the principles of rotation among Member States.

For the sake of convenience, one may consider proposing a name for the institutional framework which would reflect, as nearly as possible, the purpose and nature of the co-operation on a regional basis. The Government of Bangladesh, Bhutan, India, Maldives, Nepal, Pakistan and Srilanka convinced of the benefits that will accure from greater regional adherence to the principles. of the United Nations charter and of Non-alignment; determined to uphold respect for the principles of sovereignty, national independence, territorial integrity, non-interference in one another's internal affairs, non use of force, and peaceful settlement of disputes. They recognizing the need to accelerate the process of economic, technical, scientific and cultural development in South Asia through co-operative endeavours undertaken by the countries in the region in a spirit of good will and mutual trust and on the basis of equality and common interest and decided to establish an organisation to be known as the South Asian Association for Regional co-operation (SAARC).

The Association is open to all States in the South Asian Region subscribing to the aims and objectives embodied in the Declaration.

The Heads of the State or Government of member state shall meet once annually and may meet as aften as necessary to give directions, provide guidelines, and review the activities of the SAARC. Chairmanship of the organization shall rotate among the member countries in an alphabetic order for a term of one year commencing from the date of the Formation of the SAARC. The Summit Meeting will be attended by the highest authority of the organization. The venue of the meetings, both Summits and Ministerial, shall be the country acting as the current Chairman.

There shall be a council comprising the Foreign Ministers of member states as the principal functional organ of the SAARC. The Council shall be responsible for finalizing the recommendations for submission to the Summit Meetings, implementing the decisions of the Summit meeting, co-ordinating the various activities of the SAARC and approving the budget of the SAARC and deciding on the contributions of the Member States.

The Council shall meet as often as necessary but atleast once a year, the Council of Foreign Ministers shall establish such committees, organs, institutions and agencies as may be necessary from time to time, under the directives and guidelines provided by the highest authority of the organization. These Committees, Organs, institutions and agencies shall submit reports to the council for its consideration.

There shall be 'Secretariate of the organization headed by a Secretary General, who will be appointed by the Heads of Government of member States upon recommendation of the Council of Foreign Ministers on such terms and conditions as may be decided by the Heads of Government. The Secretary General shall be the principal executive of the organization and shall perform such functions as are entrusted to him by the countries.

President Zia-Ur-Rahman has proposed that the leaders of the South Asian Countries should meet at the Summit level to explore the possibilities of establishing a frame-work for regional co-operation. Bearing in mind the legacies of the past, it would indeed be a historic event. Barriers, both historical and emotional, will have to be scaled and lingering suspicion and distrust will have to yield place to a renewed spirit of understanding and good will. A meeting at the Summit level would be the most appropriate forum for such a major initiative in embarking on a new and challenging venture envisaged in the proposal.

## SAARC Charter

SAARC formation was completed with the adoption of its charter and the signing of the Summit Declaration of pious, peaceful intentions and plentiful promises.

We, the Heads of State or Government of Bangladesh, Bhutan, India, Maldives, Nepal, Pakistan and Srilanka:

1. Desirous of promoting peace, stability, amity and progerss in the region through strict adherence to the principles of the United Nations Charter and Non-alingment, particularly respect for the principles of sovereign equality, territorial integrity, national

independence, non-use of force and non-interference in the internal affairs of other states and peaceful settlement of all disputes.

2. Conscious that in an increasingly interdependent world the objectives of peace, freedom, social justice and economic prosperity are best achieved in the South Asian region by fostering mutual understanding, good neighbourly relations and meaningful co-operation among the Member States which are bound by ties of history and culture;

3. Aware of the common problems, interests and aspirations of the peoples of South Asia and the need for joint action and enhanced co-operation within their respective political and economic systems and cultural traditions;

4. Convinced that regional co-operation among the countries of South Asia is mutually beneficial, desirable and necessary for promoting the welfare and improving the equality of life of the peoples of the region,

5. Convinced further that economic, social and technical co-operation among the countries of South Asia would contribute significantly to national and collective self-reliance;

6. Recognising that increased co-operation, contacts and exchanges among the countries of the region will contribute to the promotion of friendship and understanding among their peoples;

7. Recalling the Declaration signed by their Foreign Ministers in New Delhi on August 2 1983 and noting the progress achieved in regional co-operation;

8. Reaffirming their determination to promote such co-operation within an institutional framework;

Do Hereby Agree to establish an organization to be known as South Asian Association for Regional co-operation,

SAARC, hereinafter referred to as the Association, with the following objectives, principles, institutional and financial arrangements[1].

## Structure of SAARC

Institutionally, the decision of far-reaching significance in the development of SAARC was, of course, the frequency of Summit and Ministerial Meetings, as suggested by the charter. Thus, the final institutional arrangement of the SAARC was as follows :

### Article I

### Obectives

The objectives of the Association shall be

(a) to promote the welfare of the peoples of South Asia and to improve their quality of life;

b) to accelerate economic growth, social progress and culturaldevelopment in the region and to provide all individuals the opportunity to live in dignity and to realise their full potentials;

c) to promote and strengthen collective self-reliance among the countries of South Asia;

d) to contribute to mutual trust, understanding and appreciation of one another's problems;

e) to promote active collaboration and mutual assistance in the economic, social, cultural, technical and Scientific fields;

f) to strengthen co-operation with other developing countries;

g) to strengthen co-operation among themselves in Inter-national forums on matters of common interests; and

h) to co-operate with international and regional organizations with similar aims, and purposes.

## Article II

## Principles

1. Co-operation within the framework of the Association shall be based on respect for the principles of sovereign equality, territorial integrity, political independence, non-interference in the internal affairs of other States and mutual benefits.
2. Such co-operation shall not be a substitute for bilateral and multilateral co-operation but shall complete them.
3. Such co-operation shall not be inconsistent with bilateral and multilateral obligations.

## Article III

## Meetings of the Heads of State or Government

The Heads of State or Government shall meet once a year or more often as and when considered necessary by the Member States.

## Artilce IV Council of Minister's

There would be a "Council of Ministers" consisting of the Foreign Ministers of the member states. It was charged with the functions of general policy making of the Association, review of the progress of co-operation under the Association, decision on new areas of co-operation, establishment of additional mechanism under the Association as deemed necessary, decision on other matters of general interest to the Association.

The Council of Ministers shall meet twice a year. Extra ordinary session of the council may be held by agreement among the Member States.

The idea for a Council of Ministers came up in the meeting of the Standing Committee (previously known as Foreign Secretary meetings) of South Asian Regional co-operation at

Male (Maldives) in February 1985. This meeting recommended the establishment of a Ministerial Council of SAARC countries to institutionalize their collective resolve to pursue mutual co-operation to launch integrated programme of action, and it was again welcomed by the Thimphu Meeting of the Foreign Ministers in May 1985, and finally adopted into the charter.

## Article V

## Standing Committee

The Standing Committee was comprised of Foreign Secretaries of all 7 countries of the region, who were basically bureaucrats. The Foreign Secretaries, right from the Colombo Meeting 11981) till the Summit (1985), were associated with each phase of development of the SAARC.

The Standing Committee was charged with the overall monitoring and co-ordination of programme of co-operation; approval of projects and programmes, and the modalities of their financing; determination of inter-sectoral priorities; mobilization of regional and external resosurces; identification of new areas of co-operation based on appropriate studies.

The Charter suggested that the Standing Committee should meet as often as deemed necessary, but at least once a year. The Standing Committee shall submit periodic reports to the Council of Ministers and make reference to it as and when necessary for decisions on policy matters. The committee was also authorized to set up "Action Committees in case of such projects which involved to set up more than two but not all the countries".

## Article VI

## Technical Committees

The Technical Committees have been set up in each area of co-operation, with the responsibility of implementing, co-ordinating and monitoring programmes of co-operation. According to Article VI of the Charter, the technical comittees comprised of representatives of all Member States. The terms of reference of the technical committee were -

(a) determination of the potential and the scope of regional co-operation in agreed areas;

(b) formulation of programmes and preparation of projects;

(c) determination of financial implications of sectoral programmes;

(d) formulation of recommendations regarding apportionment of costs;

(e) implementation and co-ordination of sectoral programmes;

(f) monitoring of progress in implementation.

The Technical committee should submit the periodic reports to the Standing Committee. The Chairmanship of the Technical Committees shall normally rotate among Member States in alphabetical order every two years. The Technical committee might also use additional mechanism and modalities, if it felt necessary. It included the meetings of heads of national technical agencies, meetings of experts on specific fields and contacts amongst recognized centres of excellences in the region.

## Article VII

## Action Committee

The Standing Committee may set up Action Committees comprising Member States Concerned with implementation of projects involving more than two but not all Member States.

## Article VIII

## Secretariat

Besides the above mentioned five-tier institutional

framework, the Charter suggested a Secretariat for the Association, and as per the decision of the Council of Ministers of the Member States, the SAARC Secretariat was set up in Kathmandu on 16 January 1987.

English shall be the working language of the Secretariat. The role of the Secretariat shall co-ordinate and monitor the implementation of SAARC activities and to servive the meeting of the Association.

The Secretariat shall comprise a Secretary General and Professional and General Services Staff, and contain an appropriate number of functional units to be called Decisions. The Secretary General shall be appointed by the Council of Ministers upon nomination by a Member State on the basis of the principle of rotation in alphabetical order. The appointment of the Secretary General shall be for a non renewable tenur of two years. He shall hold the rank and status of Ambassador.

The Professional staff of the Secretariat shall be appointed by the Secretary General upon nomination by Member States.

The Secretary Genral shall employ such General services staff as are necessary for the normal functioning of the Secretariat.

## Functions and Powers of The Secretary General

The Secretary General as head of the SAARC Secretariat, shall (i) be responsible for conducting the work of the Secretariat including co-ordination and monitoring of SAARC activities, (ii) submit staff rules and financial regulations to the standing committee for approval of the Council of Ministers, (iii) act as the channel of communication and linkage. When so empowered by the standing committee, between SAARC and other international organizations on matters of mutual interest. In doing so, the Secretary General shall be guided by the decision of the Council of Ministers that initiatives for collaboration external agencies should stem from SAARC itself based on its own determination of priorities and keeping in mind the relevant provisions of the SAARC Charter, (iv) submit the annual Budget of the Secretariat to the Standing Committee for approval of the Council of Ministers.

## Funding and Budget

Nepal as the host country shall provide the following facilities for the Secretariat;

(i) Accommodation with initial decoration and furnishing and provision of basic utilities and services including power, water, gas, air-conditioning, telephone, telex and major maintenance of the same; The accounts of the Secretariat shall be audited annually by a Panel of Auditors comprising three qualified members nominated by three Member States by rotation and appointed every year for a contract period of three weeks of the Standing Committee. The Report of the Panel of Auditors along with the annual accounts shall be submitted to the Standing Committee for approval of the Council of Ministers.

ii) Machines, equipment and vehicles for the initial stage.

The Annual Budget of the Secretariat shall contain two main components;

i) Capital expenditure, includidng all capital costs on such items as procurement of machines, equipment and vehicles;

ii) Recurrent expenditure, including all expenses associated with the running of the Secretariat during the budget year including payment of Salaries, allowances and perquisites of all Secretariat personnel, utility charges, office requisites and stationery, minor maintenance and any other regular expenses;

iii) the Annual Budget of the Secretariat shall be shared by member states on the basis of a formula agreed upon by the Council of Ministers.

### Article IX

### Financial Arrangements

The contribution of each Member State towards financing of the activities of the Association should be voluntary. Each Technical Committee should make recommendations for the apportionment of costs of implementing the programme proposed by it. In case sufficient financial resources could not be mobilized within the region for funding activities of the Association, external financing from appropriate sources might be mobilized with the approval of or by the Standing Committee.

### Article X

### General Provisions

Article X contains the general provisions as under:

(i) Decisions at all levels should be taken on the basis of unanimity.

(ii) Bilateral and contentious issues should be excluded from the deliberations.

A close analysis of the SAARC Charter approved by the Dhaka Summit made it abundantly clear that "The Charter of the SAARC was different from the SAARC Declaration of 1983 in two very significant ways. First, in underlining the principles of the regional arrangement (in Preamble as well as Article II), the expressions "non-use of force" and "peaceful settlement of all disputes" had been added. It might be recalled that these expressions (without "all" in the second expression) appeared in the "framework" of regional co-operation proposed in the initial working paper circulated by Bangladesh in November 1980.

The SAARC Charter revealed some hurdles that needed

to be crossed, if co-operation was to materialize. The principle of unanimity in the Charter for decision making is a double-edged weapon. While it assured that there is also scope for manipulation of the forum through any one member, thereby effective sabotaging co-operation. As per the Charter, contribution to the Association is voluntary and here financial resources cannot be mobilized, external sources could be tapped with the approval of Standing Committee.

The present Institutional Arrangements have been confined to the Ministry of External Affairs only, of respective countries, though the Technical Committees have included as members, the representatives of respective areas of co-operation, but they are from the low level. Hardly, there was any occasion when ministers of that field or any senior officials had joined in the discussion[2].

The present institutional arrangement has little scope to give adequate attention to the financial arrangements. As the financial arrangements, are confined to voluntary contributions, and the contributions made in local currencies, they can be utilized only in the country concerned. Even in terms of convertibility, their values are in sharp variations e.g., one Indian rupee equal to two and a half Srilankan rupees. Again, there are differences in financial year (Bangladesh-Pakistan: July-June; Bhutan-India: April-March; Maldives-Srilanka: January-December; Nepal: 16 July-15 July).

## Functions of SAARC

The proposal for a South Asian meeting at the Summit level has been generally welcomed by the Working Paper as a positive and constructive initiative, which could have a catalytic effect on the process of co-operation in the region. However, it was argued that Summit meetings generate great expectation among people and, therefore, a step-by-step approach would be more productive. Summit meetings and to be carefully prepared in advance to ensure their success. A Summit meeting presupposes that there would be serious business for the Heads of Governments and that the Heads would be able to apply their minds to those issues which could not be resolved satisfactorily at other levels. They would have a broader perspective and, what is equally important, the power of decision to resolve contentious issues. Thus, preparatory work to be undertaken prior to the Summit meeting would include preparation of the agenda, identification of the possible areas of co-operation, and chalking out the modalities of co-operation. In the process of evolving a common position on all these aspects of the preparatory work, unanimity is desirable[3].

The scholars of the South Asian region held a number of meetings and made a number of proposal that helped to provide the kind of background analysis and Information which proved to be useful to those who latter worked out the details of the new organisation under the direction of the Foreign Secretaries and Foreign Ministers of the South Asian States. At still higher level, the initiative taken by the President of Bangladesh, Zia-Ur-Rhman in May 1980 to approach other South Asian heads of states, proposing a South Asian Summit, generated the requisite interest of the policy-making agencies to try the idea, albeit after prolonged consultations resulting in substantial reformation of Rehman's proposal.

The Declaration on South Asian Regional Co-operation marked the completion of the preparatory phase and was soon followed by a fullfledged Summit of the member nations at Dhaka. In giving final shape to the SAARC, the Dhaka Declaration is an important achievement. The Heads of State's and Government of SAARC would play regional co-operation on a firm foundation and would play an important role in accelerating the pace of economic and social development of their countries, promote the objectives of individual and collective self-reliance and further the cause of peace, progress and stability in the region and the world[4]. The adoption of the SAARC Charter and passing Dhaka Declaration reflect these countries commitments to building an Institutional foundation and promote bilateral relations among the South Asian States[5].

## First Summit Conference: Dhaka 7-8 December, 1985

The President of Bangladesh, the King of Bhutan, the Prime Minister of India, the Maldives President, the King of Nepal, the Pakistan President and the Srilanka President met in Dhaka on 7th and 8th December, 1985.

The two-day inaugural SAARC Summit in Dhaka was attended by King Jigme Singye Wangchuck of Bhutan, Prime Minister Rajiv Gandhi of India, President Abdul Maummon Gayoom of the Maldives, King Birendra of Nepal, President Gen. Mohammed Zia-Ul-Haq of Pakistan, President Junis Jayewardene of Sri Lanka, besides host President Gen. H.M. Ershad of Bangladesh. The summit was preceded by a meeting of the foreign ministers of the seven countries on December 5 and of the foreign secretaries a day earlier, when the agenda for the Summit was finalized.

In this meeting the heads of states or government et seven South Asian countries, adopted a charter converting tae South Asian Regional Co-operation (SARC) into the South Asian Association for Regional Co-operation (SAARC), with an institutional frameowrk. They reiterated the principles of unanimity and avoidance of bilateral and contentious issues from the forum. Also, a Council of Ministers, consisting of the Seven Foreign Ministers, was decided upon as the policymaking organ of the Association, with the standing committee comprising the Foreign Secretaries as the body for overall monitoring and coordination of the programmes of co-operation.

The seven leaders decided to meet annually, with the next meeting scheduled in New Delhi for November 1986, and the one after, in Thimpu. The Foreign Ministers would be meeting at least twice annually, once before the Summit. The Standing Committee would meet as often as possible. A

Secretariat was also agreed upon, with the details pertaining to venue, structure, finance and functioning to be chalked out by the Council of Ministers. The study teams were also agreed upon to examine the feasibility of regional co-operation on the problems of terrorism and drug trafficking and abuse.

## Dhaka Declaration

The Dhaka Declaration reiterated the leader's resolve to co-operate regionally in their search for solutions of their common problems in a spirit of friendship and mutual understanding[6]. Reaffirming the promotion of the welfare and prosperity of their people as their fundamental goal by acceleration of economic and social development through optimum utilization of their human and material resources the leaders stressed the need for peace and security for the realisation of this objective. The Declaration underlined the leaders commitment to the UN Charter and the NAM goals, and voiced concern at the deteriorating International Political Situation, particularly in the context of escalation of the arms race with unpresented nuclear dimensions.

They will also make determined efforts towards realisation of the goals and targets of the International Development strategy and New Programme of Action for Least Development Countries (LDCS)[7]. Further, the leaders reiterated their convinction that SAARC would play an important role in accelerating the pace of economic and social development of their countries, promote the objectives of individual and collective self-reliance and further the cause of peace, progress and stability in their region and the world.

On global security, the Summit did not go beyond routine mention of "unprecedented escalation of arms race particularly in its nuclear aspect". In this context, Summit called upon nuclear weapon states to urgently negotiate a comprehensive test ban treaty leading to the "complete cessation of testing, production, and development of nuclear weapons".

An analysis of the speeches, made at the summit, shows

that several of the principles like avoidance of reference to bilateral and contentious issues and equality of the participating states were observed more in the breach than in observance. President Zia in his Inaugural Speech, while calling for agreements at the regional level for confidence building, gave a call for steps to banish nuclear weapons[8]. But this was a contentious issue and SAARC was supposed to steer clear of such issues - since India did not favour a regional approach to the nuclear ban issue. India, while calling for a comprehensive test ban treaty at the global level, had repeatedly spoken gainst a regional approach, and especially in the context of South Asia, where its effect would be to deprive India of the weapon option against China.

President Jayewardene, in his inaugural speech, said that "India, the largest country in every way, can by its deeds and words create the confidence among us so necessary to make a beginning". King Jigme of Bhutan in his speech said that in the Geo-political realities of the South Asian region "it would be unrealistic to ignore the primacy of the political factor" and that "it may neither be possible nor desirable to limit discussion in our meetings to issues of non-political natures".

Although the summit documents did not specify any areas of co-operation, the Joint Press Release issued at the conclusion of the Summit by the seven leaders identified three more areas to be brought into the fold of SAARC. It was decided to set up two study groups to examine the problem of terrorism as it affected the "security and stability of member states" and the problem of drug trafficking and abuse and to recommend steps as to how best the member states could co-operate among themselves to solve these problems. The Standing Committee was also directed to convene a Ministerial level conference on the development of women in order to identify the areas of activities and programmes for increased participation of women at the regional level. This conference took place in New Delhi in May 1986 and recommended efforts to identify specific activities relating to women in development that could be taken up by the members nations of SAARC.

It was also decided to set up a Technical Committee on women as also a monitoring cell in the SAARC Secretariat to co-ordinate the progress made in this direction.

Subsequently, the Foreign Ministers met at Dhaka from August 12-13, 1986 to review the reports and drafts prepared by the Standing Committee regarding the Integrated Programme of Action, as also meetings on International Economic Issues, women in development and ways to combat terrorism. The Joint Communique issued at the end of the Foreign Ministers meeting, which in effect became a preparatory meeting for the second Summit stressed the need for more concrete action on agreed projects and programmes and recommended setting up of a working group to make appropriate recommendations on the staffing, funding and functioning of the SAARC Secretariat[9].

### Second Summit Conference, Bangalore Nov. 16-17, 1986

The Second Summit level meeting of SAARC leaders was held ITD 'Bangalore, the Gordan City of India on Nov. 16-17, 1986, under the Chairmanship of Prime Minister Rajiv Gandhi, the atmosphere of mutual trust, understanding and appreciation of one anothers problems which was initiated at the first Summit was further consolidated in Bangalore. The Summit leaders while giving directions and guidance for the Association to grow, underlined their deep conviction that such co-operation would not only have a salutary effect on bilateral relations between the countries of the region, but also impart strength and stability to these relations[10].

Inaugurating the conference, the Indian Prime Minister Rajiv Gandhi stressed the need for peace and referred that the arms race 'distorts economies' and 'wastes resources' could be used to ameliorate the human miseries. Focusing attention on the economic problem of the region, he suggested that the national efforts should now be complemented by regional co-operation. "We must rely on our own effort and at the same time find common solutions to common problems[11].

The King of Bhutan said, "We should particularly concentrate on the problem of trade and joint economic ventures within the region. The establishment of airlinks and telecommunications among our seven countries would also enhance regional co-operation.

President Ershad said that development of common natural resources, Himalayan resources and resources of the sea could be areas of mutually beneficial co-operation Pakistan Premier M.K. Junejo, in his speech, offered Pakistan's "co-operation in any form and at any level among the SAARC countries to eliminate the threat of terrorism", and suggested a "binding agreement" to meet the challenges collectively[12]. The suggestion was not commented upon by the others.

## Bangalore Declaration

The Bangalore Declaration underlined the leader's concern at the continuing crisis in world economy which was affecting adversely the development prospects and aspirations of the developing nations. The leaders also endorsed the need for regular and close consultations and co-operation among SAARC countries in relevant inter-national economic institutions and conferences to promote their objectives, viz., enlarged concessional assistance, track liberalization, commodity price stabilization and transfer of technology.

The Bangalore Summit also considered five new areas for expanding and strengthening co-operative programmes under SAARC:

(a) the creation of Secretariat and, thus, placing SAARC on a firm institutional framework for the first time and the designation of a distinguished diplomat as the first Secretary-General;

(b) agreeing to launch a "South Asian Broadcasting Programme' covering both radio and television - a valuable instruments in rousing South Asian consciousness;

(c) stressing the need for cross fertilization of ideas through greater interaction among students, scholars and academics in the SAARC countries, while promoting people-to-people contact through special intra-regional tourism facilities;

(d) adopting an organized volunteers, programme under which volunteers from one country would be able to work in other countries in the fields of agriculture and forestry extension work;

(e) involving youth in regional co-operation by harnessing their idealism for the resurgence of the Asian consciousness which was imperative for the success of SAARC, recognising the importance of the principles laid down in the UN Resolution 2625 which, among others, required that each state should refrain from organizing, instigating, assisting or participating in acts of civil strife or terrorist acts in another states or acquising in organized activities within the territory and directed towards and commission of such acts".

The Summit leaders recognized that the children should be given the highest priority in national development planning and expressed the belief that it should be possible to ensure the end of the century that no child would die or denial development for reasons of material poverty in the family. They subscribed to the goal of universal immunization by 1990, Universal primary education, maternal and child nutrition, provision of safe drinking water and adequate shelter before 2000 A.D.

The Heads of State or Government also decided that the next meeting of the Council of Ministers would be held in

India in May 1987. They directed that this Meeting should undertake a detailed review of the proposals for the establishment of regional institutions. The member countries which have undertaken to prepare concept papers, pre-feasibility or feasibility studies on these proposals, should complete them well before the convening of the meeting.

### Meeting of Standing Committee, New Delhi, 16-17 June 1987

At the invitation of the Government of India, the Standing Committee held its eight session in New Delhi from 16-17 June 1987. The committee reviewed the progress achieved in the implementation of the Integrated Programme of Action (IPA) since its 7th session held in Bangalore in November 1986.

The committee proposed the co-operation in following fields :

(a) Health and Population Activities

(b) Rural Development

(c) Telecommunication

(d) Women in Development

The committee considered the suggestion of the Technical Committee on Women in Development for Creating a Women's Cell in the SAARC Scretariat.

It recommended that the Council of Ministers approve the following five schemes elaborated and concretised by the experts :

(i) SAARC Audio Visual Exchange (SAVE)

(ii) Organised touring among SAARC Countries

(iii) SAARC Documentation Centre

(iv) SAARC Chairs, Fellowships and Scholarships

(v) SAARC Youth Volunteers Programme

(vi) Establishment of a South Asian Food Security Reserve

Views were expressed that there was an urgent need for co-operation in the field of Mass Media, such co-operation could take a number of forms such as establishing a common SAARC News Agency, instituting an annual SAARC Award to a Journalist from the region and greater involvement of Media in SAARC.

## Meeting of the Representatives of National Planning Organization Islamabad, 11-14 Oct. 1987

The Representatives of the National Planning Organization of SAARC Countries were devoted to be following topics :

(i) In view of the adverse International Economic situation facing the region, the meeting noted the need to pool resources for long term Regional Co-operation. A consus emerged on initiatives that needed to be taken within the SAARC framework in the area of trade promotion and economic co-operation.

(ii) Under the policy instrument for Agriculture Planning, the Group were suggested area of co-operation is water Management, anti-water logging, conductive use of water, consolidation of holdings, dry-land farming techniques and bio-technology, exchange of experts and training facilities, mutual exchange of literature and varieties of crops between member countries.

(iii) There were an urgent need for countries in region to formulate energy policies and strategies in context to their development plans and develop planning modals to project demand and supply.

(iv) It was agreed that further co-operation in the sphere of Industry would need to be supported by well conceived and focused studies on a number of specific subjects.

## Meeting of Standing Committee, Kathmandu, October 29-30,1987

In pursuance of the directive of the IInd SAARC Summit, the committee undertook the First Annual Review of the situation of children in South Asia. The committee requested the Council of Ministers to recommended to the member countries that policies for the achievement of the goals of universal immunization by 1990, universal primary education, maternal and child nutrition, provision of safe drinking water and adequate shelter before 2000, accepted by the Bangalore Summit, be integrated into the National Development Plans.

The SAARC Audio-Visual Exchange (SAVE) programme were launched on November 2, 1987. The Standing Committee also recommends the schemes for the establishment of a SAARC Documentation Centre and the SAARC Youth Volunteers Programmes.

## Third Summit Conference, Kathmandu, November 2-4, 1987

The Third Summit Conference held in Kathmandu in 2-4 November 1987, considered several issues of common, both Regional and International in terms of their overall progress in the context of SAARC objectives. The leaders reiterated the need for further consolidation and realization of the ongoing activities persuate within the SAARC framework, which it was noted with satisfaction, had made substantial progress in strengthening cooperation. They reaffirmed that fundamental goal of SAARC was to promote the welfare of the peoples of the South Asia acting in to surmount the formidable challenges of poverty, and environmental degradation facing the region.

Opening the Summit, King Birendra told the leaders that terrorists were threatening peace in the region, and they should be given no room in any country within or outside its territory. He called for a spirit of give and take among member nations and asked them to oppose efforts at balkanisation of the region[13].

Mr. Rajiv Gandhi, Prime Minister of India, pointed out that the environment was an area where co-operation was indicated. Mr. J.R. Jayewardene, President of Srilanka, called for promoting trade among the countries of the region. Bangladesh President H.M. Ershad mooted a proposal to evolve a multidimentional Himalayan Water Resources Development Plan to mitigate the sufferings of people in view of the frequent occurrence of natural disasters in the South Asia Region.

King Jigme Singhe Wangchunk of Bhutan voiced deep concern over the ever expanding nuclear arsenal and called upon the two super powers to work resolutely towards global disarmament.

## Kathmandu Declaration

The Kathmandu Declaration noted the need for consolidating and expanding regional co-operation. This, it was stated, could be effected not only through growing regional complementaries and interdependence but also though implementation of more concret and action oriented programmes as also co-ordination of national policies and approaches for finding common solution to the common problems[14].

The Declaration noted with concern the structural disequilibrium in world economy and called for equitale participation of the developing countries in International Trading and Economic Systems, as also early resumption of the North-South Dialogue. Concern was also voiced at the deteriorating International political environment due to Great Power Policies of domination and Intervention as well as increased resort to use of force, pressure, economic coercion and interference. The Declaration also welcomed the understanding reached between the United States and the Soviet Union on the Intermediate Nuclear Force and called for an early conclusion of the Comprehensive Test Boom Treaty (CTBT) and the convention to ban chemical weapons.

It was decided to support every effort to conclude a treaty prohibiting vertical and horizontal proliferation[15].

The SAARC Regional Convention on Suppression of Terrorism and the Agreement establishing South Asian Food Security Reserve were also signed by the Foreign Ministers of the SAARC member states during the course of the Summit. The convention on Terrorism marked a significant break through on a problem that literally cuts across the boundaries of South Asia and is the primary concern to all SAARC countries. The convention underlined the leaders recognition of the danger posed by the spread of terrorism and its harmful effect on peace, co-operation and good neighbourly relations in the region. The convention, comprising eleven Articles, identifies terrorist offence which cannot be considered political for purpose of extradition or prosecution and seeks to take effective measures to ensure that offenders do not escape prosecution and punishment by providing guidelines their extradition.

The setting up of a Food Security Reserve albeit with a modest stock for such a populous area marks a positive move forward in cradicating hunger from South Asia, a region which remains subjected to nature's vagaries with such alarming frequency. The foodgrains reserve would be administered by the SAARC countries. Each member country is entitled to draw on the serve in the event of an emergency about which the concerned country would directly notify the other member countries indicating the amount of foodgrain required. The release, price, terms and conditions are to be determined through direct negotiations with the country concerned, while informing the Board of the deal the agreement underlines the importance and desirability of collective self-reliance with a view to promoting economic and social development in South Asia and is bound to benefit the smaller countries of the region, who find themselves constrained to procure foodgrains in the open market due to foreign exchange constraints.

New initiatives and dilemmas came to the forth at the

Third Summit Meeting in Nepal. Just before the Summit was convened, Afghanistan applied for membership in SAARC, and it was also suggested that ASEAN should be accorded the status of observer or guest. However, as the founder documents of SAARC contained no provisions for the admission of new members, observers or guests, the Summit was faced with new problems requiring resolution.

No consensus was reached on the admission of Afghanistan largely because of the conflicting stands of Pakistan (which opposed the motion) and India (which supported it). The case was a similar one in giving form to relations with ASEAN[16].

On the broader International stage, the countries of SAARC supported multilateralism and the UN system, with special stress on the principles and objectives of the non-aligned movement and its role in the world today. SAARC also saw its field of action as including South-South co-operation, as defined at the Ministerial Conference in Pyongyang. The Declaration supported the efforts of GATT (the present round of multilateral trade negotiations) and of UNCTAD, and seconded the idea to convene an International conference on money and finance for development, as suggested at the non-aligned summit to commission a study on natural disasters and the protection and preservation of the environment in a comprehensive framework.

**The Meeting of the SAARC Group of Experts For The Study of Natural Disaster and Protection of Enviornment, Kathmandu 13-15 July, 1988**

The Group of Experts concluded that natural disaster such as floods, droughts, cyclones, submersion of coastal areas due to rise in the sea level, tidal waves, landslides, mass wasting, earthquakes etc. and environmental degradation including deforestation, water-logging, salinization, desertification, soil erosion, coastal erosion, pollution and unplanned urbanization, which have an adverse impact on the region deserved careful study. The Group noted that public awareness is very important to protect and preserve the environment.

The objectives, recommended by the Group is to provide a basis for the member countries to draw up policy conclusions and recommendation and to identify areas keeping in view the potential and possibilities of evolving a Regional Plan of Action for strengthening disaster management capabilities and for the protection and preservation of the environment.

## Meeting of Planners, Kathmandu, November 1-2, 1988

The third meeting of planners from the SAARC countries was held in Kathmandu on November 1-2, 1988. The meeting arrived at the following conclusion:

(i) It was noted that the different countries of the region are at different stages of development of data base and of planning techniques. It was felt that the building up of a certain minimum base for a statistical system would be necessary for taking the National Planning processes a step ahead and also for working towards a long-term perspective for the region collectively. The areas may be taken up for exchange of experience and expertise are, system of National accounts and input-output tables, Demographic Statistics, Trade and Balance of Payment Statistics.

(ii) The Group noted that Human Resources Development (HRD) was a term of wide cannotation covering several technical areas. The Group therefore, recommends that the education, health, nutrition, child and women development, welfare of vulnerable sections, sports and youth activities, art and culture are identified as minimum components of HRD.

(iii) Regional co-operation in field of education could include, SAARC chairs, fellowships and scholarships for study in different countries for exchange of Research Scholars, University Professors, Identification of centres of excellence in Physical and

Biological Sciences humanities for development exchange and networking with other countries in the same field.

(iv) The Group noted that the manpower planning techniques in many SAARC countries are common. In this area, the beginning should be made in the exchange of information relating to techniques of manpower planning including the methods followed for determing optimal requirement of various skills. Sharing and exchange of technology, research and development experiences in adopting labour intensive technologies to optimize labour use especially in rural areas.

(v) The meeting recommended that the Technical committee select well identified, target oriented and time-bound programme for early realization of the SAARC objectives. It is recommended that each member country establish a focal point in its Planning Commission or relevant Ministry for the purpose of consolidating sectoral studies organized under the aegis of SAARC for bringing them under a long-term perspective.

To formulate effective policies, strategies and programmes relating to the human dimension in development planning in the SAARC region by the year 2000, each country could develop its own long-term national development plan with well defined vision, strategy and targets.

**Fourth Summit Conference, Islamabad, December 29-31, 1988**

The fourth SAARC Summit, held in Islamabad during 29-31 December 1988, under the Chairmanship of Ms Benazir Bhutto, Prime Minister of Pakistan, marked a turning point in the history of the world's largest and yet youngest venture in regional co-operation.

From the SAARC'S Integrated Programme of Action

with which the seven national association of South Asia began its journey at Dhaka in December 1988, to the SAARC 'Basic Needs Perspective for 2000', adopted at the Islamabad Summit in 1988 - this denotes fairly the measure of advance that the South Asian Community has registered. The SAARC has indeed raised is sights higher, and yet it would be inappropriate to call this a leap forward in economic co-operation. It is yet the first firm step towards planned economic co-operation within the seven nation.

At the inaugural meeting, virtually all the leaders addressed attention to the wide gap that still existed between promise and reality - between the modest progress SAARC had so far achieved and its actual potential. The 7 member states of the organization had common problems of hunger, poverty, malnutrition, illiteracy and underdelopment, and a common strategy to tackle these problems within a regional framework - which provided the basis for SAARC, was emphasized by all the leaders in their speeches. All of them also stressed the need to make SAARC more effective in dealing with such problems.

Benazir Bhutto emphasized that "preconceived ideas and long held strategic nations are giving way to new approaches in consonance with the economic and technological realities of today". She listed natural calamities and the menance of narcotics as the problems requiring urgent attention. She felt that regional co-operation in checking drug trade should be made more effective. "We must mount a joint effort on a worfooting to vanish this cancer from our societies", Bhutto said and proposed that 1989 be designaced as the year of a war against narcotics[17].

Srilankan President Jayewardene was gracious enough to state that India, as the dominant partner, held the key to SAARC, and that this key is in "safe and sincere" hands[18].

The Maldives President Maumoon Abdul Gayoom

referred, at some length, to the recent turbulence in his country, which he described as "a dangerous conspiracy aimed at subverting the sovereignty, territorial integrity and independence of the Maldives". He then, went on to express his "profound appreciation" to the Indian government, for having responded "possitively and swiftly" to his request for military assitence to help overcome what he called the "mercenary aggression"[19].

'The Indian Prime Minister, Rajiv Gandhi, while pressing for the inclusion of economic areas in the ambit of regional co-operation, also went farthest in seeking to alley the misgivings of any of the member countries that regional economic co-operation might mean India getting an unfair advantage at the cost of a less dominant member of SAARC.

## Islamabad Declaration

As India has advocated since the inception of the Association, there is beginning of SAARC interaction in the economic sphere. This is what the Declaration says "In this context, (the Summit) emphasized the need to progressively carry out SAARC activities within a broad framework of a long term perspective and to harmonise their efforts to ensure tangible benefits to the peoples of South Asia as a whole. Towards this end they were to the view that all member - states should identify areas of core interest in their national perspective plans or prepare such plans and consolidate them into a regional plan to be called 'SAARC 2000 - A Basic Needs Perspective', with specific target to be met by the end of the century".

A decision adopted by the Islamabad summit was to set up in Pakistan a centre for Human Resource Development, accepting the Pakistan Governments offer to provide all the facilities for it. The Secretary General has been directed to set up a group of experts from member-states to examine the proposal on the basis of a proper to be prepared by the Government of Pakistan. The group of expert is to submit its recommendations to the Standing Committee.

Yet another gain from the Summit is the creation of a special SAARC travel document which would enable Supreme Court Judges and members of Parliament of the nations to travel freely in the SAARC member states, dispensing with the need for them to procure visas. This step the summit has taken in pursuit of the objective of closer and more frequent contacts among the peoples of the SAARC.

In developing people-to-people contact, the Islamabad summit notes that the decision to involve regional NGO's or professional bodies in SAARC activities, pursuant to the direction given by the Kathmandu Declaration, was an important step forward. The Islamabad Summit had decided to declare 1990 as the "SAARC year of the Girl Child".

Islamabad Declaration has come out some new strategies: First, it had suggested a regional plan called "SAARC 2000 - Integrated plan to provide basic needs such as shelter, education, and literacy to over on billion population of the region by the turn of the century". They had called upon the member-states to identify the areas of co-interests in their national perspective plans. Second, while expressing satisfaction over the operationalization of a "South-Asian Food Security Reserve" since 12 August 1988, the ratification of the SAARC convention on suppression of terrorism by all member nations since 22 August 1988, and the launching of a South volunteers programme among SAARC countries, the leaders decided to include education as an agreed area of co-operation. Third, while urging that the expert group on "Natural Disaster and Protection of Environment" should complete its study in the shortest possible time, the leaders decided on a joint study the "green house effect" and its impact on the region.

An added attraction of the Islamabad meetings was the signing of three important agreements on non attack on each others nuclear facilities, double taxation avoidance and cultural co-operation, between India and Pakistan[20]. The leaders of both the countries took the best advantage of that occasion and informally discussed major bilateral problems.

## Gandhi - Bhutto Talks

Three rounds of talks between the Prime Minister of India and Pakistan brightened the hopes a new phase of relations between the two countries.

The Prime Ministerial parlay were resumed on Dec. 31, 1988 after the conclusion of the SAARC summit. These were followed by a plenary session at which three Agreements were signed. These related to an agreement against attacking each other's nuclear installations, avoiding double taxation and promoting cultural exchanges between the two countries. The agreement were signed by the Foreign Secretaries of two countries, Mr. K.P.S. Menon and Dr. Humayun Khan.

Meanwhile, the possibility of greater "flow of information and news" between the two countries was considered bright. In their talks, the two Prime Ministers explored steps for a reduction of troops on their common border. There would also be exchange of visits of representatives of educational, literacy, artistic, sports and journalists associations and organizations and participations in conference, symposia and seminars.

The Cultural Agreement also carried a clause barring the two nations from any misrepresentation of facts about each other's country, especially in text books relating to history and geography.

The agreement also promised exchange of visit of sports team between the two countries[21].

## Special Meeting of The Group of Co-ordinators For Studies on Trade Manufactures and Services, Colombo, 31 March to 1 April 1989

In pursuance of the directive of the fourth SAARC

Summit at Islamabad, the Group considered proposals to identify any, specific areas where co-operation may be feasible immediately in the fields of trade, manufactures and services. The Group noted that the studies being undertaken in keeping with the agreed objective, terms of reference, methodology, funding and common format for the country-wise studies would provide the basis for identification of measures and specific work programme to promote co-operation among the SAARC countries.

The Group emphasised that there should be a much greater level of exchange of economic and commercial information among Trade and Industry circles in the member countries which would facilitate regional co-operation.

### SAARC Meeting of Expert of Energy Modeling Techniques, New Delhi, June 8-9, 1989

A meeting of experts from SAARC member countries in the field of energy modeling techniques was held in New Delhi on June 8-9, 1989.

The Planning Commission in India uses a core Model for perspective planning supported by a number of sub-Models related to important areas such as agriculture, industry, etc. these Models incorporate growth, equity and self-reliance as the primary goal of macro-economic planning. The knowledge and experties that has been gained through these efforts could be shared among the countries in the region.

Exchange of ideas among the countries in the region would go a long way in promoting Regional Co-operation in this important area.

The meeting underlined the vital importance of development and promotion of Energy Modelling as a tool for planning. The ground agreed on the need to exchange information and expertise on energy modeling techniques used in the member countries.

Special emphasise may be placed on Rural Energy, specially exchange of information relating to Data, the methodologies and the experiences in the applications of renewable energy technologies.

With a view to ensuring regular exchange of knowledge and information in the area of energy modelling techniques, the Group recommended that an effective networking may be developed among the institutions and agencies working in this field.

To this end, each member country may draw up a list of Institutions and Agencies for circulation through the SAARC Secretariat.

**Fifth Summit Conference, Male, Novemeber 21-23, 1990**

The Male summit was especially significant because four Heads of States those of India, Pakistan, Nepal and Srilanka were meeting jointly for the first time. On the other hand, the other three countries representative had attended all the meetings so far.

This summit held at a time of videspread internal turmoil and greater uncertainity about this regions place in the world than these countries have known in decades. Four of the seven regional nations- India, Pakistan, Nepal and Srilanka- have new government, all born of controversy and violence to one degree of another of the remaining three, Bhutan and Bangladesh have been consumed by political unrest.

One measure of the atmosphere leading meeting of South Asian Association for Regional co-operation is that it was repeatedly postponed. The summit could not meet in the year 1989 on account of the India - Srilanka tensions. Srilanka refused to take its turn in holding t he meeting because Indian troops were on its soil. Again t he collapse of the Indian government caused a last minute delay of two days. Srilanka had tried to stall the Kathmandu Summit making the unilateral air dropping of food parcels to stranded Tamils in Jaffna a major issues.

The Male Summit began on a high note of political s Pakistani systems with the new Prime Minister declaring that the difficulties On SAARC) experienced last year are a matter of the past and we can look forward to every increasing co-operation within our association[22].

Though there is a decision to schew bilateral contentious issues from the ambit of SAARC discussions, there was evidence of this attempt even at November 1990, Male Summit when the Prime Minister of Pakistan, Mr. Nawaz Sharif, with the tacit support of the former Bangladesh President, Lt. General H.M. Ershad, argued for a "Binding SAARC Agreement" on Regional Nuclear Non-Proliferation - a Mini NPT. General Ershad spoke of a larger, Saner system of collective security with back-up regional arrangements. The Indian Prime Minister, Mr. Chandra Shekhar, was able to neturalise these proposals by pointing out that with the end of the cold war, the global and regional situations had drastically changed and the "contemporary world context itself demands intensified economic co-operation among South Asian Countries".

The Male Summit can be regarded as marking a turning point of SAARC activity, provided the decisions taken there are implemented in earliest. The provision is very important because the inability of the SAARC to translate rhetoric into action has effectively nullified the sense of euphoria generated at the birth of the Association. A number of projects secured endorsement at the Summit level but reamined unimplemented in practice. This is more due to the absence of political will at the top levels and less due to institutional weaknesses.

However, a new wave of hope appears to have been generated at Male. First, the Summit largely at the persuation of India, decided to extend economic co-operation to the core areas. India's Foreign Secretary Muchkund Dubey rightly emphasised at the meeting of the foreign secretaries of the SAARC countries that the "SAARC will acquire a self-sustaining momentum only when hard core economic co-operation becomes integral to its activities, Mr. Chandra Shekhar has said, "Economic co-operation among the South Asian countries has its own logic and compulsions. The farmers of the SAARC Charter, therefore, displayed foresight and wisdom in not making such co-operation contingent upon the solution of bilateral problems"[23].

The fifth Summit itself got under way after the recitation of a verse from the Holy Koran. Reference to Islamic fraternity dominated the inaugural session. While Nawaz Sharif described the host country, Maldives, as a "Fraternal Muslim country;' Ershal made a significant reference to an initiative by six Muslim Countries of Asia to try and resolve the raging Gulf Crisis. Ershad at the same time sought to enlarge the scope of discussions under the SAARC umbrella to cover the Gulf Crisis as a SAARC agenda item.

These new ideas aired at the inaugural session were, in a sense, prefaced by the host President, Abdul Gayoom's fervent plea to all the SAARC countries to speed up the enactment of national level legislation to make the SAARC convention on suppression of terrorism operations without delay Gayoom suggested that environmental issues, including global warming and sea level rise (which poses a threat to Maldives) should be studies in depth in time for the sixth summit likely to be held in Colombo next year[24].

Mr. B. Wijetunga, the Prime Minister of Srilanka, also made a poignant reference to the security of small states. King Jime Singye Wangchuk of Bhutan called for more bilateral meetings at the SAARC Summits to dispel misunderstandings and apprehension that might sometimes affect relations between the member countries[25].

## Male Declaration

The declaration[26] adopted by the leaders of the SAARC at Male Summit called for the withdrawal of Iraqui forces from Kuwait and the restoration of its legitimate government. It highlighted the intrinsic relationship between disarmament and development and urged the early conclusion of a comprehensive test ban treaty. The SAARC nations anxiety over the Gulf developments in understandable since they are among those hit the hardest by the crisis and stand to suffer further in the event of continuity of an armed conflict there. With large numbers of the world's poor and impoverished within their fold the SAARC nations have reason to feel reassured by the progress of disarmament and the formal conclusion of the cold war. Naturally they will feel more secure if there is a formal nuclear test ban treaty.

The political outlooks of the SAARC nations remain too diverse to make economic co-operation wholly smooth, but the leaders present at Male recorded their good intentions. Thus, the aspiration to mobilise regional resources for collective self-reliance in the region found expression in the Male declaration.

India circulated at the Summit a report on a proposed regional council for financing development institutions. It said the member countries now have the skills to deal with new instruments of international finance. They should therefore try to exploit long-term investment opportunities among themselves. The suggestion to develop preferential trade arrangements among them by eliminating trade barriers and discriminatory practices is also one the SAARC nations can put to good effect in future.

The Summit saw the signing of the convention to combat Drug Trafficking in the region, along the lines of the convention on the suppression of terrorism signed earlier. There were agreements on their subjects like exploring the modalities for setting up of a regional fund for financing joint venture projects in cottage and small scale industries and handicrafts. It was decided to set up a Nucleus Human Resource Development Centre in Islamabad, a Regional Documentation Centre in New Delhi. The visa exemption facility for travel within the region, earlier applicable only to Supreme Court judges and member of Parliament, it to be extended to heads of national academic institutions. One of the important decisions, as part of the people-to-people contact programme, related to increased exchanges among South Asian media personnel. The idea of a SAARC Tourist Exchange Programme, initially with 500 tourists a year under relaxed visa regulations was also proposed[27].

The decision to search for new avenues of regional interaction undertaken at Male is to be welcomed not only because such a move would reduce tensions but also pave the way for a more earnest implementation of projects in the new areas of agreement like mass media, biotechnology and environment. It is needless to say that the South Asian region is in ferment and there is greater need now than before for forging new bonds among the countries which constitute the SAARC. The sole impediment in the past in the way of purposeful translation of ideas into reality has been the mutual distrust factor.

The Male Summit provided Prime Minister Chandra Shekhar an opportunity for meet his Pakistani counterpart, Nawaz Sharif, and leaders of other SAARC nations.

**Sixth Summit Conference, Colombo, December 21, 1991**

The sixth Summit conference at the level of the Heads of States or Government of the South Asian Association for Regional co-operation was held at Colombo on 21 December, 1991. The Sixth Summit was originally scheduled to be held on 7th November 1991. But could not held because of the Bhutan Kings inability to attend owing to domestic problems and India insisted on a full quorum and decided to abstain from the abortive summit. Sri Lanka President Ranasinghe Premadasa openly alleged the underhand of India in the Bhutanese King's absence from the Summit. He along with the Pakistani Prime Minister, Nawaz Sharif vociferously that in future, no single member on a small group would be able to veto it by boycotting any meeting.

The SAARC Chairman, Ranasinghe Premadasa has underlining the need for SAARC countries to embark on greater co-operation in trade and the economic field. He said that Sri Lanka had removed the controls which constricted economic activity and sought to attract foreign investment, technology inflow and joint ventures. Premadasa added that SAARC could work towards creating a South Asian Preferential Trade Area. Then only could SAARC envisage the eventual establishment of a South Asian Economic Community (SAEC)[28].

Mr. P.V. Narasimha Rao, Prime Minister of India, urged a "collective economic-security system' for the SAARC members. He also talked of the need to relax trade barriers in the region. The long term vision of SAARC must include the removal of internal barriers and "the free movement of good services, capital and peoples throughout SAARC"[29].

The one day meeting in Colombo will hopefully set the precedent for the future. It drew attention to the possibility of "negative consequences" for the South Asian region of new economic groupings that have or about to come into existence as a result of new developments in the International political arena. This apart, a new found urgency among the member states is to be noted/ that is, not to be left behind, as the new international order gets evolved and regional and economic groupings make raid strides in technological and trade fields.

The Summit leaders directed the Foreign Secretary level standing committee to meet in a special session to collate and study all proposals and comments regarding adaption of a more business like approach in the conduct of SAARC proceedings. The committee would submit its report to the Council of Ministers.

## Colombo Declaration

At the end of a seven-hour business like sixth Summit of the SAARC, the leaders adopted an eleven page Colombo

Declaration and also decided to work towards the global objective of "Shelter for all by the year 2000"[30]. In the Colombo Declaration, the leaders covered a wide range of issues besides economic co-operation, suppression of terrorism and drug trafficking, security of small states, establishing a regional development fund poverty alleviation and welfare of women and children[31].

They have declared their commitment to the liberalization of trade in the region through a step-by-step approach in such a manner that all countries in the region share the benefits of expansion equitably, the inter-governmental Group (IGG) has been asked to study the Sri Lankan proposal for the establishment of SAARC Preferential Trade Arrangement (SAPTA) by 1997. Even before, such a wide agreement take concrete steps, however small in themselves, to increase the flow of intra-regional trade.

A high political note of consensus marked the Summit declaration on such diverse issues as the establishment of a South Asian Commission on Poverty Alleviation, the examination of a proposal to set up a Regional Development Fund and the need to keep economic development at the centre of International Attention in the current debate on primacy for Human Rights and Democracy in the Third World countries[32]. Reinforcing their collective political World Countries will to keep SAARC afloat in the gathering International storm over the creation of a New World Orders of the leaders from India, Pakistan, Bangladesh, Sri Lanka, Nepal, Bhutan and the Maldives decided to hold the next Summit, the seventh in a series, in Dhaka next year.

With bitterness over the postponed SAARC Summit lingering and with Pakistanis studied attempt not to let the dust over it settle, the Colombo meeting of the seven South Asian leaders could barely hope to be anything other than what it turned out to be a jamboree held under political compulsions. The factor that led to the postponement of the

November Summit suggests that the lack of political trust would continue to hinder the association's progress. Because, the SAARC remains precariously fragile, none of its seven members would take upon itself the balance of doing anything to cause its collapse.

Even while SAARC is trying to figure out the mechanics of regional economic co—operation, it could usefully promote the habit of working and acting together by evolving common positions of issues figuring on the International Economic Agenda. The ASEAN Ambassadors in Brussels, for example, get together to co-ordinate their positions vis-a-vis the European community, and their SAARC counterparts could do the same.

Likewise, mutual interaction can be promoted, as is sought to be done by setting up a Commission of "Eminant Persons" to review progress of poverty alleviation. Improved people to people contacts would be very useful in promoting regional awareness but this is best achieved by freeing travel from government imposed restrictions which are specially severe in the Indo-Pakistan case. The hope will prove to be well founded if the Member States realise that being together would help them immensely in an emerging world which might see ruthless trade wars and protectionism. Instead of a political enquiry into its members conduct, the SAARC will do better to concentrate involving mechanisms that could protect its members economic interest against powerful global entities.

On drug trafficking, the declaration said the leaders noted with satisfaction the increasing regional co-operation in combating the problem of drug trafficking and drugabuse. While expressing satisfaction at the signing of the SAARC Convention on Narcotic Drugs and Psychotoric Substances at the fifth SAARC Summit at Male, they urged the member countries which had not yet done so to ratify the convention for its entry into force.

On International Economic Issues, the SAARC countries emphasized the importance of assessing the nature and extent of International Economic Inter-dependence and of the need for reviving the North-South Dialogue. They noted the recent developments that had rapidly transformed the International development relationship, deeply affecting the prospects for the economies of the seven SAARC countries.

On the World political situation, the Declaration said the changing power structures, in International Relations and the reduction of confrontations and tensions, particularly among the super-powers, had contributed to the receding of the threat of nuclear confrontation.

Pakistan re-iterated its desire to turn South Asia into a Nuclear Weapon Free Zone and proposed consultations among USA, Russia, China and India to resolve the issues. On Nuclear Non-Proliferation, he said his country was willing to enter into any International, Regional, or bilateral commitments in this regards[33].

The Colombo Declaration reported no consensus on the subject. It said the Heads has asked the SAARC Secretary General to set up a pannel of experts for a feasible study on establishing a South Asian Development Fund, "taking into account the views of all member states". In the Declaration the Heads of State also welcomed the setting up of a SAARC Fund for Regional Projects (SFRP).

The issue of the developed world imposing linkages between development aid and Human Rights made its first appearance in a SAARC Declaration. But there were some old favourites, like the SAARC Head's affirmation of their faith in "non-use of force, the peaceful settlement of disputes and non-interference in each other's internal affairs[34].

**Seventh Summit Conference, Dhaka, April 10-11, 1993**

The two-day Summit held in the Dhaka, Capital of Bangladesh after two successive postponements, served to demonstrate the resilience of the SAARC process and its inherent ability to surmount unexpected difficulties.

Bangladesh Prime Minister Begum Khalida Zia said in her Inaugural Address, that Co-operation in SAARC had developed along many new and important dimensions. We cannot however, deny that some of our activities were diffused and had limited impact. They are yet to touch the life of our common people whose welfare is our foremost objective. Our priorities for the future are very clear, Endemic poverty of our people constitutes a major challenge for all our countries. Our countries must also gradually move towards making appreciable progress in hard-core economic areas. Economic co-operation can only be ignored by our countries to our detriment[35].

Mr. Nawaz Sharif, Prime Minister of Pakistan, raised the issue of "freedom and self-determination of the oppressed and subjugated peoples" which diplomatic circles regard as a veiled reference to the Kashmir issue. Without specifically mentioning any particular area, Sharif said freedom and self-determination of oppressed and the subjugated peoples must be accepted as the collective responsibility of the entire International Community[36].

Nepalese Prime Minister Koirala, in the balanced presentation, said that it is a matter of satisfaction that our association has withstood wide scepticism that preceded and accompanied its establishment. It has overcome many obstacles. It has asserted and re-asserted itseif through vicissitudes, and has acquired an element of irreversibility. But the recent events in the subcontinent which necessitated the postponement of this annual session warn us that this irreversibility is fragile. Confidence in the future of our Asscoation is under strain in the climate of fear and suspicion[37].

The comenting role played by Nepal was one of the notable aspects at the Dhaka Summit. And there is a specific underlying development which made this possible. Koirala was able to speak from the crest of democratic upswing in Nepal, just when in other areas of the subcontinent, whether it was India, Pakistan or Bangladesh, the forces of religious fundamentalism cast a shadow which had an ill-effect on the SAARC.

There is an element of satisfaction at the poise and grace with which India acted during the SAARC, in a lucid presentation pointing to the changing global economic. political climate and the importance of the SAARC- "our collective economic strength and weight as a mega- market of billion consumers" - the Indian Prime Minister pointed to the way for word for the South Asian Community without projecting India as a big brother.

## Dhaka Declaration

At the end of Summit, SAARC leaders adopted Dhaka Declaration and have agreed on the following points :

(a) Eradication of poverty in South Asia, preferably by the year 2002 A.D. through an agreed Agenda of Action;

(b) Necessary steps should be taken to being the first round of trade negotiations to exchange trade preferences among member states under the Agreement on SAARC Preferential Trading Arrangement (SAPTA) ;

(c) Determination to continue in future the practice of intra-SAARC consultations on matters of common concern, as was done prior to the United Nations conference on Environment and Development;

(d) Agreement that co-operation among Member States should be strengthened, both through sharing of experiences and in other practical ways, to enhance their capacity to deal with the population problem;

(e) Endorsement of the "Colombo Resolution on Children" adopted by the Second SAARC Ministerial conference on Children held at Colombo in September 1992;

(f) Designate (1994 as the "SAARC year of the Youth" to address the problems of the youth and focus on the 'broad theme of youth and development;

(g) Adoption of the Regional Plan of Action for the Disabled Persons;

(h) Endorsement of the recommendation of the Council of Ministers for the establishment of an Inter-Governmental Group (IGG) on South Asian Development Fund (SADF) on an ad-hoc basis;

(i) An Expert Group of the Member States will examine the various requests for observer status at SAARC/ SAARC Meetings to all its aspects on the basis of a working paperto be prepared by the Secretariat and make appropriate recommendations to the Nineteenth Session of the Standing Committee;

(j) Acceptance of the offer of India to host the Bight SAARC Summit in 1994[38],

The signing of the framework agreement on South Asia Preferential Trade Arrangement (SAPTA) at the Seventh SAARC Summit at Dhaka marks the first major step towards expanding trade among the member - nations after eight years of pious exhortations for increased regional economic co-operation. Initially Pakistan, was opposed to signing the SAPTA framework agreement. But with other member-nations keen on going ahead with it so that a political direction could be given to the much-talked about trade arrangement. Islamabad found itself isolated and gave it.

## Eighth Summit Conference, New Delhi, 2-3 May, 1995

The Delhi SAARC Summit took place at a time when the political climate in South Asia was particularly bad. The Chairperson of SAARC, Begum Khalida Zia, had visited all SAARC countries for consultations except India. The Prime Minister of Pakistan, Benazir Bhutto, chose not to attend the Summit and instead Pakistan was represented by its President,

Farooq Ahmad Khan Leghari.

The Eight Summit Conference of the SAARC Head of States or Government was held at New Delhi on 2-3 May, 1995. The Summit began with discordant notes being struck by Pakistan, Nepal and Maldives who demanded that bilateral issues be discussed at this forum if it was to resolve "unsettled political issues in the region" and be effective in alleviating poverty, combating malnutrition and improve the quality of life of the people. Pakistan came close to calling for a change in SAARC charter which precludes discussion of bilateral issues.

Pakistan President Mr. Leghari observed, the fact is that our Association has not taken off. The reason is not far to seek. The suspicions and insecurity generated by the unsettled political issues in our region stand in the way of SAARC moving forward at the pace that it should be.

While the new Chairman of SAARC, Prime Minister P.V. Narasimha Rao and Sri Lankan President Chandrika Kumaratunga focussed on the development of a Free Trading Area in the region being a common goal of SAARC, the King of Bhutan, Jigme Singye Wangchuck, favoured member countries having the will to make use of the informal bilateral consultations during summits to resolve existing problems and difficulties. Maldive's President Gayoom warned that mutual suspicions among members could jeopardise the future of the decade old SAARC. There was a need to remove these suspicions. Bangladesh Prime Minister Begum Khalida Zia regretted that member countries were still "deeply divided".

Referring indirectly to differences with India on the Nuclear issue, President Leghari called upon the South Asian leadership to "rise above local considerations and enter into a regime to banish for ever the spectre of nuclear weapons from the area[39].

SAARC members had ratified the SAARC convention on Narcotic Drugs and Psychotropic Substances. Indian Prime

Minister P.V. Narasimha Rao said that this provide a very effective instrument at the regional level to fight the menace of drugs and illicit drug-trafficking which needed to be stamped out[40].

Fortunately for South Asia, in spite of the complex political situation prevailing in the region, there are strong forces that tend to favour regional co-operation. New economic policies that have been adopted by them have given rise to opportunities to link up with global economy. Such opportunities can be exploited better in the framework of regional economic co-operation. Finally, all the countries in the region have to race formidable challenges arising from the emerging co-existence of globalism and growing Regionalism in North America, Europe, and the Asia Pacific region.

Another important development is the increasingly important role which the Non-Governmental organizations (NGOs) are playing, particularly SAARC Chamber of Commerce and Industry, SAARC Law and others that deal with issues such as poverty, sustainable, development, environment, education, human rights, women's employment etc. Some non-governmental bodies had also sponsored several scholarly studies highlighting the cost of non-co-operation and the benefits of co-operation[41].

## The Delhi Declaration

The Delhi Declaration of the eight Summit has called for an International Convention prohibiting the use or treat of use of Nuclear Weapons under any circumstances, and strongly deplored acts of terrorism spreading in and outside the region.

The proposed convention should be negotiated by the conference on disarmament which should also undertake discussions for the complete elimination of all Nuclear weapons within a time-bound framework, the declaration suggested. Reiterating the need to fulfill the Internationally Agreed Aid targets for the developing countries and least developed countries, the declaration underlined the need for exceptional finance to facilitate implementation of economic reform programmes in SAARC countries.

The Declaration wanted a review of the membership of the UN Security Council with a view to reflecting the increased membership of the United Nations and promoting a more equitable and balanced representation.

The most important stress was on eradication of poverty in South Asia. The year 1995 has been declared as the "SAARC year of Poverty Eradication". A programme of Action has also been adopted. The leaders reiterated the commitment to eradicate poverty in South Asia by 2002 A.D.

An important decision was the direction given by the SAARC leaders that all necessary steps should be taken to facilitate ratification of agreements on SAARC Preferential Trade Arrangement (SAPTA) and its operationalisation by the end of 1995 as mandated. The Ministers have agreed that the full and timely realisation of the benefits of regional economic co-operation required the implementation of other related measures such as the removal of para-tariff, non-tariff and other trade control barriers within the specific time frames; and the eventual progression to the creation of a free trade area in the region.

The Committee on Economic Co-operation (CEC) has been requested to focus upon the promotion of intra-regional investment and the establishment of joint ventures at its forthcoming session and to formulate specific measures for the attaintent of the objectives of the SAPTA Agreement.

Sub-regional Economic Co-operation has been considered as a means to accelerating the SAPTA process. A tripartite study would be undertaken by the governmental, business and academic sectors on expanding intra-regional trade, including informal trade.

Commerce Ministers are expected to meet in December 1995 or early 1996 in order to give impetus to intra-SAARC trade under the SAPTA Agreement. The proposal of establishing a SAARC highway would be pursued to expand intra-SAARC trade.

A three-window South Asian Development Fund with the merger of SAARC Fund for Regional Projects and SAARC Regional Fund and a third window for social development and infrastructural development has been approved[42].

While recognising the need to improve, expand and deregulate markets to promote sustained economic growth, the declaration felt it was essential to mitigate any negative features created by the market forces and make all efforts to ensure the markets were friendly to the poor.

In the field of environment an important advance is the commitment of the leaders of implement at all levels national bilateral, regional and global - programmes for the protection and preservation of the environment and prevention of its degradation.

For the first time there is reference in the SAARC document to reaffirmation of commitments by leaders to safeguard the basic interest of workers. This has been followed by the leaders calling upon countries to refrain from effecting trade barriers in the guise of promotion and protection of workers rights. Conditionalities on Inter-national Trade, whether as a 'social clause' or as the 'environmental clause' has been deplored.

A most important decision was the decision of the Council to meet in a commemorative session to mark the First SAARC Decade during its sixteenth session in India in December 1995. The theme of the session would be "SAARC-vision for the Second Decade".

The Declaration reiterates that co-operation in the area of Science and technology should be accorded high priority and call for accelerating the process of establishing netweorking arrangements in the fields of bio-technology, genetic engineering, energy modelling techniques and low cost housing and building technologies.

In the field of International co-operation, notworthy development is the authorisation given to the Secretary General to sign an inter-institutional co-operation agreement between SAARC and the European Union and also a Memorandum, an understanding with the UNDP and UNDCP (United Nations Drug Control Programme). The Chairman of the Council of Foreign Ministers has been requested to continue his consultations with the Troika of the European Union. He has also been asked to continue to maintain contact with ASEAN in order to promote cooperation between SAARC and ASEAN. The SAARC Secretariat has been asked to continue interacting with the Asian Development Bank (ADB). The Council has agreed that SAARC should explore the possibility of establishing co-operation with APEC and keep itself abreast of developments regarding the Association of Indian Ocean Rim Countries (AIORC).

Positive anticipations about the New Delhi Summit related to business like decisions regarding the enlargement of intra-regional trade. India certainly has gone overbroad by offering concessional customs duties for SAARC partners on 106 items. Pakistan, by contrast, has set down 53 categories for concessional imports but limiting 29 among them to the four least-developed countries (LDCS) of the region-Bangladesh, Bhutan, Nepal and Maldives. All this represents an extremely tentative step towards mutual trade promotion in the region.

## Delhi Declaration of South Asian Parliamentarians: New Delhi, 8-10 August 1995

The Parliamentarians of the SAARC countries participating in the conference of South Asian Parliamentarians towards the solidarity for Equality, Development and Peace, New Delhi, Aug. 8-10, 1995.

The conference has adopt the Dhaka Resolution on women passed at the SAARC Ministerial Meeting on Women: Towards the Fourth World Conference on Women in Beijing, held at Dhaka, 29-30 July 1995.

The conference recognise that the heavy burden on women in the SAARC Region, arising from "women-improvident maternity" i.e. births to teen-age girl at late age, of high parity, or those too close together, that deliberate the women's physical health and general well-being, they urge special emphasis to the improvement of the reproductive health within the framework of improved basic health services.

The Parliamentarians recognises that the most effective way to address population concerns in through investment in the human person, particularly the women and girl child.

Because of lack of education, early and excessive children, early marriage, denial of social status, women are locked into low paid, unskilled occupations in the unorganized factor. Women are generally paid lower wages than men for performing similar work.

They recognise that externally controlled media netweork and their unbridled spread, specially the electronic media, is commercialising and distorting the very fibre of the social framework with particularly negative influences on female life. The denial to women of the ownership and control of land, property, and other economic contribution to the gender gap in economic well-being, social status and empowerment, especially in largely rural economies, such as those of South Asia.

They declared that all forms of violence against women and girls, including domestic and family abuse, should be liminated. The conference has called the Parliamentarians of the region to eradicate poverty in absolute terms, particularly because it has persistently resulted in increasing burden on women. It emphasises that National as well as International efforts for eradication of poverty be reinforced in all possible manner. For successful implementation of the Platform for Action, they call for categorical commitment from the International community, multilateral financial institutions and national Governments for the new and additional resources required[43].

## Nine Summit Conference, Male, 12-14 May, 1997

The Nine Summit conference of the SAARC heads of States of Governments was held at 12-14 May, 1997. The Summit has shown that the constructive ideas whose time has come cannot be held in abeyance. The economic integration of the region is a development necessity. Hundeer leads to anger and social revolt. The collective wisdom of the assembled 7 countries decision-makers has rightly foucssed the regional community's attention on socio-economic upliftment through a clear-cut three tier poverty eradication programme[44].

For the first time in many years, the meeting between Prime Minister Inder Kumar Gujral and Prime Minister Nawaz Sharif at Male has brightened the prospect of SAARC, whatever the fears. It looks as if the organization may acquire some meaning the stumbling block, Kashmir, may matter less. The two have discussed the problem but as a bilateral issue.

India nost only agreed to sell the 50,000 tonne of Sugar to Pakistan but also allowed its highways by road most of it from Paghwara to Lahore. SAARC's dictum to he one another came to the fore and the core problem of Kashmir was pushed into the background[45].

They agreed to set up a hotline between New Delhi and Islamabad and direct their Foreign Secretaries to evolve a "Comprehensive Mechanism to address all outstanding issues" between the two countries including what the Pakistanis discribe as the "core issue of Kashmir".

The SAARC leaders agreed for the removal of all trade barriers and structural impediments by advancing the deadline of four years from the earlier agreed goal of SAFTA by 2005.

Prime Minister I.K. Gujral lobbied hard with SAARC Heads of State and governments during the three day Summit to advance the deadline for the implementation of SAFTA from 2001 to 2005.

The Summit leaders also responded positively to Gujral's proposal for the vision of transforming SAARC into an ultimate economic community for the region. However, his suggestion for the launching of studies to develop the concept of economic community was not incorporated in the 12 Page Male declaration.

## Male Declaration

The Male declaration said that the political dialogue would help "foster good neighbourly relations, relieving tensions and building confidence as means to promoting peace, stability and accelerated social and economic co-operation in our region".

The SAARC leaders affirmed their commitment to combat terrorism and drug-trafficking in the region and emphasised the urgent need to enact ennobling legislation to implement the SAARC regional convention on suppression of terrorism and narcotic drugs and psychotropic substancies.

The summit called for the expansion of the UN security council on the principle of sovereign equality of States and on equitable geographical representation.

Ninth Summit concluded on 14th May with the South Asian leaders agreeing to convert the South Asian Preferential Trading Arrangement (SAPTA) into a South Asian Free Trade Area (SAFTA) by 2001. The summit adopts a lofty Declaration calling for for eradicating poverty in the region by the year 2000[46].

Answering a question about the slow process of SAFTA during the past three years under which the member countries could finalise only 2000 of the 6000 items for tariff concessions, Gayoom said : "All our efforts would be made to complete the process soon". Gayoom also welcomed Gujral's proposal for South Asian Economic Community (SAEC) and said that the idea would be pursued after attaining the goal of SAFTA.

The leaders also called for the formation of a group of eminent person (GEP) for comprehensive appraisal of SAARC. The group was asked to develop long-range vision and formulate a perspective plan of action including a SAARC agenda for 2000 and beyond, and submit it to the next Summit to be held at Colombo in 1998.

Besides making a special mention of enhancing the political co-operation the ninth SAARC Summit Declaration also expressed its commitment to eradicate poverty in South Asia by 2002 and directed the Finance Ministers of the member-countries to meet often to give further impetus to the process. The leaders of India, Pakistan, Bangladesh, Sri Lanka, Nepal, Bhutan and the Maldives in the sumit declaration said SAARC's steps to promote social and political awareness in the region had brought positive contribution to the issues of gender equality and empowerment of women.

The Declaration called for renhanced co-operation to bring the women into the mainstream of socio-economic development in the region. The leaders also conducted a mid-decade review of the SAARC Plan of Action on the Girl Child and expressed their determination to accelerate efforts to reduce malnutrition and mortality rates and raise the literacy rate.

The leaders also called for urgent implementation of the recommendations of the SAARC regional study on the "Green House Effect" and its impact on the region and regional study on the cause and consequences of natural disasters and protection and preservation of the environment.

It also directed that the next meeting of SAARC Environment Ministers meeting to be held in Male on 1997, should consider the feasibility of dawing up a Regional Treaty on Environment. On tourism the SAARC leaders noted that the organised tourism in South Asia had not yet achieved its full potential and asked the officials to initiate appropriate measures to promote people-to-people contact.

The leaders also resolved to hold the next Summit in Sri Lanka instead of Nepal and accepted the request make by President Kumaratunga in this regard. Sri Lanka wanted to hold the Summit next year in connection with its 50th year of Independence[47].

## An Appraisal

SAARC was established with the objectives of achieving through regional co-operation certain economic and cultural goals, and in the process generate mutual trust and understanding conducive to peace and stability in the region. Therefore, one of the foremost needs appeared to be the creation of a political environment conducive to regional co-operation for the fullest development of the economic potential of the region through the collective pursuit of the SAARC goals. Ten years in SAARC, after its formal launching at the Dhaka Summit in December 1995, were far too short a period for an objective and dependable evaluation of its performance.

The SAARC process, culminating in the first summit during its fairly long gestation period (extending over 5 years), successfully encountered many impediments and survived many crises. The care and competence, with which the spade work in the form of joint studies was carried out in the identification of the areas of co-operation including in the Integrated Programme of Action, laid a sound foundation for the final launching of SAARC at the Dhaka summit in December 1985, that is, within a period of only five years from the date of the mooting of the idea in 1980 by Bangladesh.

The major problem appeared to be intellectual and perceptional. How to break away from the shackles of some of the doctrinaire security ideas and perceptions, which historically proved to be a source of tension, strain and conflict in inter-state relations and obscured the enormous potential of the region in achieving collective self reliance.

The Annual Summits of SAARC and the more frequent meetings at the level of Foreign Ministers and other Ministers provided a unique opportunity for confidence building among the SAARC countries, which was one of the central ojbectives actuating the concept of SAARC.

Though SAARC as an organization enters its second decade, South Asia in many ways remains a basin of darkness in the spheres of political, social and economic co-operation. There has been much acclaim at the Governmental as well as intellectual and public level for South Asian co-operation and for making SAARC the collective voice of South Asia. However Summits held so far have been mired either by narrow bilateral issues or have been exercises in purely cosmetic gestures.

There has been limited success in the sphere of economic co-operation upon which hinges the very viability of SAARC. It is clear that an economically integrated SAARC will be in a better bargaining position vis-a-vis other regional trading blocs as well as in its dealing with the North, than individual nations. It should be mentioned that the South Asia Preferential Trade Agreement (SAPTA), specially meent to boost regional trade, was approved in Dhaka. It could not get off the ground mainly because of Pakistan's suspicions and susceptibilities. It is a good augur that in the Eighth Summit in New Delhi, a consensus was evolved among the member countries to operationalise SAPTA by the end of the year and a list of items for duty concessions was also finalised. In the. Ninth Summit at Male, they agreed to converted SAPTA into a South Asian Free Trade Area (SAFTA). This agreement could make up for the past failure and open up new vistas of co-operation for the countries of the region.

## References

1. Documents, 'Charter of the South Asian Association for Regional co-operation; World Focus, Vol. 10, 1989; p. 23.

2. K.P. Saksena, "South Asian Regional Co-operation"; A paper presented in the Seminar organized by South Asia Division, School of International Studies, Jawaharlal Nehru University, New Delhi, 1985, pp. 12-14.

3. P.K. Mishra, 'South Asia in International Politics", pp. 49-50.

4. S.D. Muni, op. cit., p. 242.

5. A.Z. Hilali, 'Genesis of South Asian Regionalism', Asian Studies, Vol. XII, July-December, 1994, pp. 29-35.

6. Dhaka and Bangalore Summits: Declarations and Joint Press Releases (Kathmandu; Secretariat of SAARC), pp. 175 .

7. Ghulam Omer, no. 17, p. 98.

8. Bangladesh Times (Dhaka), 8 Dec. 1985.

9. SAARC Perspective, May 1987, p. 12.

10. SAARC Perspective, May 1987, p. 12.

11. Indian Express (New Delhi) 17 Nov. 1986.

12. Ceylon Daily News (Colombo) 18 Nov. 1986.

13. Hindustan Times (New Delhi) 3 Nov. 1987.

14. South Asia Journal, 1988, Vol. 2, no. 1, p. 11.

15. Nancy Jetly, no. 9, p. 70.

16. Times of India (New Delhi), 3 Nov. 1987.

17. Nation (Lahore), 30 December 1988.

18. Pakistan Times (Islamabad) 30 December 1988.

19. Muslim (Islamabad) 31 December 1988.

20. Times of India (New Delhi), 1 January, 1989.

21. Asian Recorder, Vol. 35, 1989, p. 20-30.

22. Indian Express (New Delhi), 22 November 1990.

23. S. Viswam, World Focus, November - December, 1990, p. 7.

24. Indian Express (New Delhi), 22 Nov. 1990.

25. Hindu (Madras), 22 November, 1990.

26. SAARC Documents: Milestone in Evolution of Regional Co-

operation in South Asia (December, 1989 - July 1991), Vol. III (Kathmandu, SAARC Secretariat), pp. 11-20.

27. S. Viswam, World Focus, November-December, 1990, p.8.
28. Hindu (Madras), 22 December 1991.
29. The Sunday Times (New Delhi), 22 December 1991.
30. National Herald (New Delhi), 22 December, 1991.
31. The Sunday Times (New Delhi), 22 December, 1991.
32. Hindu (Madras), 22 December, 1991.
33. Asian Recorder, 1992, Vol. 38, Page No. 22149,
34. The Statesman (New Delhi), 22 December 1991.
35. Bangladesh Observer (Dhaka), 11 April, 1993.
36. National Herald (New Delhi), 11 April, 1993.
37. Patriot (New Delhi), 11 April 1993.
38. SAARC Newsletter (Kathmandu), Vol. 6, No. 5 and 6, 3 January - June, 1993, p. 2.
39. Time of India (New Delhi), 3 May 1995.
40. Indian Express (New Delhi), 3 May 1995.
41. Kant Kishore Bhargava, (Former Secretary General of SAARC), Delhi SAARC Summit: Malaise and Progress; Mainstream, Vol. 33, June 24, 1995, p. 5.
42. Ibid., p. 6.
43. Link, November 6, 1994, Vol. 36-37, pp. 30-31.
44. Attar Chand, "SAARC: A Suitable Forum" Janata, Vol. No. 12, June 8, 1997, p. 7.
45. Kuldip Nayar, "Musings A Male Summit, Gujral-Sharif talks and SAARC", Mainstream, 35 (24); Vol. XXV, No.23, 24 May 1997, pp. 5-6.
46. Ibid, p. 6.
47. Attar Chand, "SAARC: A Suitable Forum"; JANATA, Vol.32, No. 12, June 8, 1997, p. 8.

# 5

# Achievements and Prospects

SAARC was established with the objectives of achieving through regional co-operation certain economic and cultural goals, and in the process generate mutual trust and understanding conducive to peace and stability in the region. Therefore, one of the formest needs appeared to be the creation of political environment conducive to regional co-operation for the fullest development of the economic potential of the region through the collective pursuit of the SAARC goals.

The several important facts that seemed to augur well for the SAARC achievements that the SAARC progress, culminating in the first summit during its fairly long gestation period, successfully encountered many impediments and survived many crises.

The apparent indicators of SAARC's progress appears to be positive. The first Foreign Secretary level meeting held in April 1981 in Colombo decided to include only five areas of co-operation namely, agriculture, rural development, communication, meteorology, health and population. The number of the areas included in the Integrated Programme of Action (IPA) has since grown considerably and now covers sports, arts, culture, postal services, tourism, transport, education, scientific and technological collaboration, women and child development, suppression of terrorism, control of drug abuse, environment, disaster management, food security, audio-visual exchange and planning experiences, etc. Many SAARC fellowships and chairs have been established. A consensus has been reached on the definition of terrorism and a convention on steps for its prevention has been signed. A common stand to be adopted on North-South issues has been agreed upon. A decision has been taken to built up a reserve stock of food grains in every member country for Regional Food Security System. Agreement has also been arrived at to foster people-to-people contact among the countries of the region by providing fillip to regional tourism and general promotion of co-operation in the field of art and culture. These are indeed impressive achievements.

The long list of area of co-operation in the SAARC charter still exlude the core areas of co-operation in trade, finance, money and industry. Through the acceptance of South Asian Preferential Trade Agreement (SAPTA) does appear to be a step forward towards the eventual formation of Regional Trading Block[1].

The progress made by SAARC is marked by some notable concrete achievements, such as :

## Agriculture

A Technical Committee on Agriculture recommends the setting up of some centre on Agriculture Information, problems of Soils and Rice Research[2]. The committee has recommended priority action on genetic engineering and bio-technology, homestead vegetable production, food avail-ability and nutritional balance.

The committee has recognized the need for a Regional Information system for effective promotion of co-operation in the field of Agriculture among member countries and proposed to the Standing Committee for the establishment of a SAARC Agricultural Information Centre (SAIC) in Bangladesh. The Council of Ministers accepted the recommendation of the Standing Committee in 1986 and SAIC would established in Bangladesh. SAIC is the first Regional Institution established under aegis of SAARC to review the progress of ongoing activities in the area of the publication of the Directory of Agricultural Institutions, Directory of Technological Scientists and Technologists and the Directory of ongoing Research Programme in SAARC countries.

SAARC Agricultural Information Centre (SAIC) collect information on current Agricultural literature, on-going research and development projects, research and development institutions, education and training opportunities and resource persons in various fields of agriculture through the member countries focal point in the network.

SAIC has select, analyses and process regional agricultural documents useful to regional users, produce bibliographies, directories of regional importance, provide selective dissemination of information, copies of documents, micro-fiche of non-conventional (or published) literature generated from the region and function as the regional centre for South Asia and have access to the International Information systems such as AGRIS, CARIS, CABI etc. and other Regional Agricultural Information Systems such as AIBA, FANDINAP- NFIS, etc.

It has developed information system using modern techniques to provide various services, such as Selective Dissemination of Information (SDI), Referral, Bibliographies, Directories, Current Awareness Service including provision for arranging translation of information into English from selected languages through a pannel of translators.

## Rural Development

In the field of Rural Development, SAARC countries has agreed to exchange of national literature and data, particulars of experts, training facilities, etc.; they identifying national referral sources, national research and training institutions and also holding workshops focused on the priority concern alleviating rural poverty to be organised respectively by Bangladesh, Indian and Srilanka.

The Technical Committee on Rural Development has suggested programmes relating to poverty alleviation, women in development, sustainable rural development, environment and technology transfer.

The SAARC leaders have accorded high priority to the alleviation of poverty in all South Asian countries and decided to establish an Independent South Asian Commission on Poverty Alleviation. The commission, since then, has held five sessions in different member states and finalised its report at its to meeting in Colombo on October 26 to November 1, 1992. The commission has in its report alanysed comprehensively various aspects of poverty, identified shortcomings in past efforts to alleviate poverty and has suggested clear cut strategies to address this chronic problem. It is interalia, put forward "A Plan for the Poor". The report of this study has recommended a concrete and practical "Agenda for Action" for eradication of poverty in the member countries within a ten-year time from, i.e., by the year 2002[3].

## Meteorology

In the field of Meteorology, South Asian countries has adopted the short term, Medium and long term projects. Short-term projects has included a Regional Research Award, Training in various fields of Meteorology, exchange of Scientists, organisation of seminars, establishment of National Data Centres, Post-Meteorological offices for obtaining data from ocean areas and Environmental Pollution Monitoring Stations. Its also included Meterological inputs for harnessing alternative sources of energy; such as solar and wind energies and Scientific studies relating to weather forecasting, climatology and its applications and instrumentation.

The medium and long term projects has include establishment of a Regional Meteorological Research Centre, establishment of a Regional Test and calibration facility, creation of Regional Data Bank, Organisation of Research Flight Facilities for probing cyclones, and Network of Drafting and Anchored Buoys in Oceanic regions.

That items of work, relating to improvement of existing telecommunications, establishment of National Data Centre, Post Meteorological offices and Environmental studies may be implemented by the member countries within their own resources except for assistance on a short-term of experts. Some countries have, however, indicated the extent to which training facilities could be provided free of cost.

The Technical Committee on Meteorology has suggested that member countries should increase their activities relating to the International Decade for Natural Disaster Reduction. The Committee recommends the setting up of a Regional Meteorological Research Centre and a number of National Data Centres in different countries with a provision of training and mutual learning on a regional basis.

The countries has agreed to setup a SAARC Meteorological Research Centre (SMRC) in New Delhi. This would meet a long-left need of the region for developing an effective system for prevention of disaster caused by floods, cyclones, draughts with hit some part or the other of the region almost annually.

## Tele-Communication

The Technical Committee on Tele-communication has recommended priority action in regard to human resource development and management. It is noteworthy that the quality of Inter-country links, such as ISD, automatic telex and bureau-fax services, have improved substantially and most member states have introduced media-independent tariff and common collection charges.

SAARC working Group on tele-communication and recommended that the data and information should be exchanged on a regular basis among the countries of the region. The member countries should be identify the specific requirements of experts and training in specialised subjects and also the facilities available, which could be extended to participants from other countries. Seminar programmes of the various countries should be circulated directly amongst the participating countries well in advance and Regional Seminar has been organized at least once in two years.

The member countries circulate their surplus production capacity available with them from time to time and cost free training and accommodation are provided to trainees of the participating countries.

The member countries has agreed for the establishment of Regional Software Centre, setting up of a Regional Satellite System, Co-operation in the field of Research and Development and setting up of Regional Data Network.

## Science and Technology

In the field of Scientific and Technological Co-operation, SAARC countries has adopted short-term and long-term programmes. The regional countries are offered short-term on-the-job training facilities for a certain number of personnel of member countries in their Science and Technology Institution. They exchange the services of experts, research scientists in the identified areas. Subjects for organizing Regional Seminars/Workshops are selectively chosen and the events carefully planned so that maximum benefit is derived from them by the member countries.

The Technical Committee on Science and Technology recommends holding of regional workshop on various subjects of relevance, improving the infra-structure for exchange of information and for training of technical manpower[4].

In Scientific and Technological co-operation "needs and

resources" can only be assessed when proposals for joint projects in specific fields are considered. Research and Development projects are adopted in field of Development of low cost infant foods, Bio-gas technology, repair and maintenance of scientific instruments, information and utilization of agro-waste products for the production of energy, Bio-technology and Micro-electronics.

## Save

The SAARC Audio-visual Exchange (SAVE) programme launched in November 1987 is already in operation. Its importance is greater than commonly realized in as much as it could play in increasingly useful role in widening and deepening South Asian consciousness among the peoples of the region with its far-reaching impact on a meaningful regional co-operation in other areas.

## Health and Population

The Technical Committee on Health and Population Activities has suggested the possibility of understanding immediate and long-term, well-identified, target oriented and time bound programmes in primary health care, tuberculosis and leprosy, water and sanitation and nutrition of children.

The member countries are agreed to exchange of Experts, training facilities and scholarships, supply of drugs, vaccines and equipments, strengthening and expansion of Laboratory and production facilities in respect of diarrhoeal diseases, tuberculosis, leprosy, Malaria and rabies.

The Working Group on health and Population has suggested that there are need for organizing seminars and workshops where experts from various disciplines could exchange ideas or experiences and acquaint themselves with the developments in their respective fields and programmes drawn up for combating the identified diseases.

The SAARC Tuberculosis Centre (STC) is the second

regional institution after SAIC. The centre is to be located in Nepal. Since the financial and other administrative arrangements have been worked out, the STC has now become functional.

The Governing Board of the SAARC Tuberculosis Centre (STC) met at its annual meeting in Kathmandu on January 7-8, 1997 and reviewed progress in the implementation of the activities of the centre during 1996. It also finalised the work programme of the centre for 1997-98.

The meeting noted that a number of activities aimed at prevention and control of Tuberculosis in the region, were organized during the year. They relate to human resource development, creating greater awareness of TB Control measures, co-ordination of TB control measures, co-ordination of TB control efforts between the government and private sector, improving the quality of anti-TB drugs. A number of personnel involved in TB control programmes were introduced to pilot Demonstration Areas and greatly benefited through participation at joint - training programmes, covering relevant areas. The SAARC Tuberculosis Centre quarterly Newsletter provided important information on its activities and developments in the areas of TB control.

The short-term activities in the work Programme for 1997-98 include a training programme on strengthening IEC activities with special emphasis on TB and HIV to be held in India, a workshop relating to research on TB and HIV in SAARC countries, a five-day training of trainers for TB Programme Managers in the Maldives, and a seminar on Socio - Anthropological Research studies in the field of Tuberculosis conducted in the member countries. In addition, a number of important studies are expected to be conducted during the year 1997-98.

The meeting was Inaugurated by Minister for Health of Nepal, Arjun Narshigh, K.C., who in his Inaugural address highlighted the need for enhanced co-operation among the Member States for prevention and Control of Tuberculosis and expressed confidence that collective and concerted efforts from member countries will be able to help in tackling this problem effectively[5].

## Transport

It is considered that the countries desirous of obtaining assistance on getting their man power trained in the context of improving transportation facilities in their countries and the assistance of countries in the region work out long - term plans for the development of different modes of transport in their countries. The exercise would not only help the country in spelling out their needs of manpower clearly and precisely, but would also help in channelising their available resources meaningfully and effectively.

SAARC countries are agreed for the co-operation on the field of rural roads designs, construction, agencies for execution, costs and funding, operating, construction and maintenance of roadways, national highways, state highways and rules, procedures, driving, regional driving licence stipulations for the safty on roads.

They are also agreed for the exchange of expertise in design engineering of railway bridges, maintenance of tracks, railway electrification; and establishment of regional training centre for this purpose.

In the field of Air transportation, areas of co-operation are the collection of route navigation and facilities charge, flight caliberation, flight safety including search and rescue, common/central Air worthiness requirements, common way for major repairs, overhaul and certification of Air worthiness for at least common type of Aircraft and common practices and procedures.

They are also agreed for design of special river-crafts suitable for this region, construction and repair of such river-craft, study on hydrographic air ways, development of parts and ship-building. The SAARC countries are exchanged the data, information, experts and training facilities in the field of transportation - Land, Water and Sea-areas.

## Postal Services

The member countries noted that expertise in various fields of postal services was available in the countries of the region and agreed that the member countries would exchange information on the available expertise.

Some of the countries of the region are in a position to offer technical assistance like fellowships, consultancy services, and equipment to other postal administrations of the region. The member countries are exchange available data and information on postal affairs. They are considered the proposal for establishment of a regional Data Bank and study centre.

They recognised that it would be appropriate to issue a commemorative postage stamp to highlight the solidarity among the people of South Asian countries.

## Education

The Technical Committee on education has emphasized in its programme the networking of its educational institutions. It has suggested immediate priority in the field of woman education, universal primary education, literacy, post-literacy and continuing education, educational research, Scientific and Technical education, education for underserved areas and groups, and distance education.

The SAARC countries have also taken initiatives on certain other issues of vital importance to the region such as elimination of gender-disparity and empowerment of women, and eradication of illiteracy. Some programmes have also been undertaken by the member countries in these areas. All the above measures taken by the official institutional framework of SAARC are expected to contribute to strengthen relationship among the SAARC countries.

The countries are agreed to establish SAARC Documentation Centre (SDC) of Indian National Scientific Documentation Centre (INSDOC), New Delhi, India, for the databank on economic and social indicators of the member countries.

## Children in the SAARC Agenda

The advantages for the seven countries of South Asia in co-operating in trade, on tourism or sports are more readily understood than the logic of coming together on behalf of children. Every five years or so, the SAARC member-states meet to review what is being done and what needs to be done at let children development to their full potential. Designated Ministers, together with advisers on primary health, basic education, nutrition and child protection, from each country consult with their counterparts and collectively decide on measures to tackle common problems. These Ministerial Resolutions come up for ratification by the Heads of States or Governments at their Summit meetings.

## Rawalpindi Resolution of Children of South Asia

Two Ministerial conferences were held - the first in New Delhi in 1986 and the second in Colombo in 1992 to reach a regional consensus on sustainable measures to realise the rights of children to survival, development, protection and participation. In the New Delhi Conference Member States agreed on the concept, framework and direction for mutual co-operation on child-related issues. Heads of State or Government at the Second SAARC Summit in Bangalore in 1986 placed children on the SAARC agenda under which they recognised that the meeting of their needs was the principal means of human resource development, and decided that children should, therefore be give the highest priority in the national development planning.

Pursuant to the commitment made by member states to children, to consolidate and to build on the progress made so far, member states decided to hold the third SAARC Ministerial conference on children in Rawanpindi, Pakistan on 20-22 August 1996.

The conference has realise the need to develop and move towards a vision for the SAARC region for the year 2000 and beyond; and note that the main features of the changing situation of children include significant progress towards the survival goals, such as reduction of infant and child morality.

At another level, guineaworm disease has virtually been eradicated. Polio can be eradicated with a stronger and more co-ordinated efforts. Control of diseases like neonated telanus, measles, diarahoea and acute respiratory infections is strengthening, while old diseases like malaria, hepatitis, TB and new ones like HIV/AIDS are a causes for concern.

The conference has noted children requiring special protection - the girld child, working children, children in urban slums and without shelter children exposed to sexual exploitation and voilence, disabled and displaced children and those caught up in socio-political and armed conflicts. An urgent need to accord political priority to investing in and strengthening an enabling environment in terms of health and nutrition, knowledge and skills, protection and active participation of children and women. Gender justice and equality as key aspirations for children being pursued collectively by Government as well as voluntary and community based organizations.

In this context, alliance for children, built around the SAARC, concept of 'Government Community Partnership' can provide a conductive environment for child development. The conference decided to launch a comprehensive nutrition initiative in South Asia, supported by measures such as : adoption of the SAARC Code on Breast Feeding and young child nutrition and supplementation of micro-nutrients like iron, iodine and vitamin A; adoption of a SAARC convention of Iodized Salt.

The conference has decided to initiate SAARC Immunisation Day, Synchronising National Immunisation Days, supported by other child health strategies, with the aim of making South Asia polio-free and eliminating neonatal tetanus and measles deaths by the year 2000. The political commitment further needs to be strengthened and reflected in recognising that children's and women's development are insparably linked, the emerging support for the Convention on the Elimination of all forms of Discrimination Against Women (CEDAW) in the region should be give impetus, and taken furth inter-sectoral, integrated local planning to meet the multiple needs of children.

In this vision, it should be possible, during the first decade of the new century to attain sustainable measures to realise the rights of children to survival, development, protection and participating[6].

The participants are agree on and resolve to achieve the set of goals by the year 2010; i.e. establish a sustainable social and physical environment in both rural and urban settings, reduce under 5 child morality rate to below 35 per 1000 live births and maternal morality rate to 100 per 100,000 live births, enable all children of primary school age to complete school at the required level of learning, child labour in bondage or otherwise, working in hazardous occupations should be eliminated by the year 2000, and the vision beyond the year 2000 includes the realisation of a deeper sensitivity to human rights in general and women's rights and child rights in particular, at the level of the state and the society. In the context of the vision beyond the year 2000, they recommend that the year 2001 - 2010 be declared as "the SAARC decade of the Rights of the child".

The participants are agree on and resolve to achieve the set of goals by the year 2010; i.e. establish a sustainable social and physical environment in both rural and urban settings, reduce under 5 child morality rate to below 35 per 1000 live births and maternal morality rate to 100 per 100,000 live births, enable all children of primary school age to complete school at the required level of learning, child labour in bondage or otherwise, working in hazardous occupations should be eliminated by the year 2000, and the vision beyond the year 2000 includes the realisation of a deeper sensitivity to human rights in general and women's rights and child rights in particular, at the level of the state and the society. In the context of the vision beyond the year 2000, they recommend that the year 2001 - 2010 be declared as "the SAARC decade of the Rights of the child".

## SAARC Decade Action Plan for the Girl Child 1991-2000

The Islamabad Summit (1988) gave a collective call to the member-states to observe 1990 as the "SAARC year of the Girl Child". In order to maintain the momentum of sustained action required to help uplift the girl child, the Male Summit (1990) decided that the years 1991-2000 be designated as the "SAARC Decade of the Girl Child".

The definition of the girl child includes the adolescent girl, and the relevant age group for the Decade Plan is 0-20 years, as the problems faced by the girl child in Bhutan, Maldives and Srilanka relate more to adolescence and equal opportunities for social morality and work participation, while in Bangladesh, India, Nepal and Pakistan problems confronting the girl child start even before her birth and continue into her adult life.

The guiding principles of the SAARC Decade Plan of Action for the Girl Child are :

(i) The equality of status of the girl child will be ensured through special opportunities for her growth and development of her full potential as individual and as a citizen in her own right;

(ii) without prejudice to the integration of the goals for the girl child with the goals for 'children and

Development' in the 1990s, her situation demands formulation of additional goals and strategies that are sensitive to her specific and multiple needs;

(iii) the socio-cultural discrimination prevailing against the girl child in South Asia, as revealed by demographic and socio-economic indicators, requires change in social attitudes and behavioural practices in relation to the development opportunities for her.

The SAARC Decade Plan of Action for the Girl Child identifies the goals of elimination of gender disparities in infant and under-five child morality rates. It emphasis on raising the present mean age at marriage by at least two years and postponing the first pregnancy till after the age of 20. In respect of malnutrition, the goal is that of reduction of severe and moderate malnutrition among under five children by half; the SAARC goals also stands for elimination of gender disparity in this regard.

The Decade plan has identified three basic aspects, namely, health and nutrition, education, and the problem of early marriage and motherhood.

Under health and nutrition programme, by the year 2000, it plans for reduction of infant and under-five morality rate for girls by one-third the 1990 rate or to 50 and 70 per 1000 live births respectively whichever is less and also reduction by half of severe and moderate malnutrition among girls under five years and starting among girls between 12-18 years.

Under the education and literacy programme, it hopes to achieve by the year 2000 - universal access to opportunities for basic education to girls under 16 years; completion of primary education by at least 80 per cent of girls of primary school age; and literacy for at least 80 per cent of out of school adolescent girls.

As regards marriage and motherhood, it is proposed to ensure by 2000 - the reduction of the proportion of early marriage among girls, raising the present mean age at marriage by at least two years and postponement of first pregnancy till after the age of 20, thereby contributing to reduction in the rates of population growth as well as infant and maternal morality.

For implementing the Plan of Action, it suggests the periodic analysis of the situation and status of girls in relation to national development policies and programme, family incentive schemes such as "Food and Education" and similar support, funding a variety of activities under the Decade Plan based on a policy decision to substantially increase hard core investment of public resources for basic human development and linkages with sectoral programmes of health, education, nutrition and economic development.

In short, the basic objective of the SAARC Decade Plan of Action for the Girl Child (1991 - 2000) is to strengthen mutual exchange of knowledge and support among the member-states in order to reach the common goals for the upliftment of the girl child throughout South Asia[7].

## Tourism

The Technical Committee on Tourism has recommended the appointment of a consultant for making a detailed study to formulate strategies for joint promotion of regional tourism and to look into the joint participation of SAARC member states in important tourism fairs. The committee has also agreed to the proposal for establishing free conventibility of national currencies for tourists of SAARC countries travelling within the region.

An aim of SAARC's activities is to promote more and closer people-to-people contact and increased interaction among them in the seven countries. The adoption of the scheme of visa-less travel for a certain class of people and organized tourism within SAARC countries has done little for realisation of this aim. On the country, every SAARC country now enforces the requirement of a visa for travellers from other member countries[8].

## SAARC Convention on Suppression of Terrorism

The "SAARC Regional Convention on Suppression of Terrorism" was another notable achievement in the violence - ridden region. The measure was likely to contribute significantly to peace and stability in the region through co-operation among the member-states in combating terrorist activities, thus, adding an important political content to the SAARC Programme.

The signing of the regional convention on "Suppression of Terrorism" was rushed through at the Kathmandu Summit, 1987. It finally came into operation from August 22, 1988, following its ratification by the member states9. The convention in its present form consists of eleven articles. By adopting this convention, the member-states have resolved "to take effective measures to ensure that perpetrators of terroristic acts do not escape prosecution and punishment by providing for their extradition or prosecution".[10]

The point about the conventions referred to is that they require specific offences to be established as Crimes under the municipal law of States which are parties to them and they lay down cases where the contracting states may exercise their jurisdiction.

According to Article l(e) of the SAARC convention such acts as "murder, manslaughter, assault causing bodily harm, Kidnapping, hostage - taking and affences relating to firearms, weapons, explosives and dangerous substances when used as a means to perpetrate indiscriminate violence involving death or serious bodily injury to persons or serious damage to property" constitute terrorism. But again this has been placed under the law of the concerned contracting state.

The convention creates obligations for the : contracting parties to change the existing extradition treaties and to formulate any further extradition treaty in line with the provisions of the convention (Art. III). Given the fact that the SAARC member states are interrelated out by extradition treaties, the fate of any extradition request, even after the convention's coming into effect, is highly questionable.

This flow in Art. III necessitated and paved the emergence of Art. IV, which provides that in cases when a State does not comply with the extradition request "shall submit the case without exception and without delay, to its competent authorities, so that procecution may be considered".

Extradition of an alleged offender found in the territory of a contracting state is also "subject to national laws" of that state (Art. VI). This clause subject to national laws - puts the convention under the national law of the state concerned, although one of the main objectives of any such International Treaty is to unify the material laws of contracting states or invent new laws where ever such are nonexistent.

The priority and prominence of the national laws accorded to in the convention is sufficient to manifest that till now there is no common understanding within SAARC of the object or the subject of a terrorist act falling within the scope of international law, there is supposingly a considerable difference in the definition of the corpus delicti of an act of terrorism, no indication of the range of persons entitled to protection from an act of terrorism, or of the grounds for such protection, or of its ways and means.

At least some of the above mentioned shortcomings of the convention have to be removed if the convention is to play the role enumerated in the Preamble. Depending on the corpus delicti and its social danger, co-operation of SAARC countries for the purpose of suppression of terrorism may proceed along the following lines:

(i) Unification of the standards of national legislation in respect of offences that amount to terrorist acts, and punishments thereof;

(ii) Creation of convention machinery of legal co-operation in the presence of an International Element within the corpus delicti;

(iii) Creation of a system of regional criminal justice implying the functioning of a SAARC criminal court or other ad-hoc courts and Tribunals for prosecution of terrorism cases;

(iv) Introduction of several punishment for terrorism (e.g., long terms of imprisonment, death sentence etc.[11].

But the actual experience does not generate much hope in this regard take for instance, the case of the Bombay blast in March 1993. The exchanges between the Indian and Pakistani Prime Ministers on the repartriation of the blast suspects showed there is little meeting ground between the two sides, even in a straight forward as this one, where Pakistan promises to co-operate in tracking down the Bombay blast case, but does nothing. The SAARC is therefore, destined to just remain as tense as they are[12].

## SAARC Law

Outside the official, framework of SAARC, initiatives have also been undertaken by professional bodies to promote mutual understanding and co-operation in the region. One is the establishment of SAARC Law which is an association of persons engaged in legal profession in all SAARC countries.

SAARC Law was established in October 1991 in Colombo with a view to promoting closer co-operation, exchange of ideas, dissemination of information and an empathetic understanding of the problems of the region among lawyers, judges, juristis and law teachers in the SAARC countries. SAARC Law has been set up a non-governmental organization of experts and prepares detailed research studies on specific issues concerning SAARC countries. The Secretariat of SAARC Law has been established in Colombo. It is important to note that a SAARC Law has a involvement of the judiciary, practicing lawyers and academicians. The SAARC Law has so far held four annual conferences in different member countries which have provided substantial opportunities for all the members of the legal community, including the judiciary of the apex courts of all the SAARC countries to discuss legal issues and forward the recommendations to the member countries.

As is well known, all commercial and economic activities of individuals and enterpreneurs and their interaction among themselves or between them and other institutions like government, banks and other agencies are governed by the legal system prevalent in each SAARC country. Hence increased levels of economic and commercial activities among SAARC countries can be successfully accomplished only if the enabling legal framework facilitates such activities. Thus, legal reforms might be necessary in some areas or in some countries to promote intra-regional trade and investment expansion. SAARC Law can play a very useful role in this respect. The leaders of the SAARC countries at the Eight Summit Meeting held in New Delhi in May 1995 have recognized the effective role that could be played by the SAARC Law in fostering closer co-operation[13].

## Economic Achivements

Economic co-operation is central to the success of any regional association. Since the official beginning of SAARC in 1985 economic co-operation in core areas has been made a "Self-denying ordinance"[14] and kept out of the deliberations of SAARC agenda. The need for promoting trade co-operation featured among the concerns of official circles in the Bangalore Summit (1986) of SAARC Heads of State and Government. In the Islamabad Summit in 1988, a more concrete step was taken as a regional study on "SAARC Trade, Manufactures and Services" designed to identify various hindrances to trade expansion within SAARC, was commissioned. The study made some practical recommendations aimed at inclusion of trade and other economic areas into the agenda of co-operation in SAARC[15].

For the purpose of economic co-operation, SAARC countries are agreed on the following arrangements :

**(i) SAARC Fund for Regional Projects (SFRP)**

SFRP has been set up for the development of Regional Projects. For the success of Integrated Programme of Action, as also other activities, funding modalities need to be worked out. In this context, a SAARC Fund for Regional Projects with a funding of $ 5 million has been in operation since 1992. Contributions have been received from the nodal Development Financing Institutions (DFIS) of member states. The objectives of the fund is to provide funding for feasibility studies for viable joint ventures between two or more countries of the region. In this context a number of project ideas have been shortlisted by the council for further investigation.

This fund is to be managed by a Regional Council of Development Financing Institutions of the SAARC Member Countries. A proposal to establish a South Asian Development Bank has also been made and it is being examined.

**(ii) South Asian Development Fund - (SADF)**

A South Asian Development Fund (SADF) was established initially as a panel of experts under the Chairmanship of the Foreign Minister of Bhutan, at Sixth SAARC Summit. After exploratory consultations, an 'inter-governmental group of South Asian Development Fund' was established to define its size, resources, structure and operational modalities, and its relationship with the existent SAARC Fund. At the second meeting of the Inter Governmental Group (IGG), a recommendation was made that the SADF may be established through the merger of SAARC Fund for Regional Projects (known as the SFRD) and the SAARC Regional Fund (SRF). This was approved at the Fifteenth Session of the Council of Ministers which was held in New Delhi in May 1995. At the Sixteenth Session of the Council, the report of the expert working group was unanimously adopted, thus establishing the SADF.

The SADF is to function as an umbrella fund with three 'windows', to be managed and operated by a Governing Board, which is to identify specific regional projects. Thus, there is a 'window' for identification and development of projects (WIDP), and another one for 'institutional development projects'. These projects have to located within the SAARC region and be of interest to two or more countries. Non-regional donors would also be approached for co-financing of projects[16].

### (iii) SAARC Chamber of Commerce and Industry (SCCI)

The national chamber of Commerce and Industry from the seven countries have formed the SAARC Chamber of Commerce. This should help in the proper exploitation of the opportunities provided by the liberralised economic policies, entailing on increased role for the private sector.

The SAARC chamber was inaugurated in 1994 with its headquarters being located in Karanchi. The SAARC chamber can become an effective instrument to promote trade and economic co-operation among the member countries. The SAARC Secretariat has recognised the role of the SAARC Chamber[17].

The SAARC Chamber of Commerce and Industry (SCCI) would contribute positively to enhancing co-operation in the crucial areas of trade and economic relations. The Standing Committee has further requested the Secretary General to facilitate increased interaction among federations/ associations of Journalists, news agencies and mass media of member States. The speakers of Parliaments of SAARC member States met at Kathmandu on November 15, 1992 and formally launched the Association of SAARC Speakers and Parliamentarians. Moreover, several Non-Governmental Organisations representing architects, accountants, lawyers, insurance companies, etc., have shown keen interest in getting SAARC recognition[18].

Since the 8th SAARC Summit important steps have been taken to expand trade and economic co-operation under the organization. In 1996, the first meeting of SAARC Commerce Ministers and the first SAARC Trade Fair were both held in New Delhi.

There is a growing realisations in official circles that all stands to gain through the pooling of resources, attaining standardisation, enhancing efficiency in the industrial enterprises of the region, to produce competitive products[19].

The fifth SAARC Suthmit (Male, Nov. 1990) emphasised the need for evolving measures for establishing joint ventures in the field of Cottage industries and handicrafts to promote collective self-reliance in the region. A group of experts has identified priority area and made several action oriented recommendations for marketing and export promotion, design development, procurement and supply of raw materials, skill upgradation, transfer of technology, enterpreneurship development.

## (iv) SAPTA

The trade and transit barriers and other economic regulations and restrictions along the border pose a different set of problems, resulting intense functional conflicts across the borders. Unlike the European Countries, the boundaries in the SAARC region function more as an economic barriers than a link between nation-states. In recent years following the path of developed countries effort for a frontierless Europe, of borderfree America on the pattern of EFTA and NAFTA, the member countries of SAARC have made efforts for more economic co-operation among them and formed the South Asian Preferential Trading Arrangement (SAPTA)[20].

The initiative towards establishing SAPTA was taken during the sixth SAARC Summit in Colombo in December 1991. A high level Committee on Economic Co-operation (CEC) of Commerce Secretaries was established in order to institutionalize economic co-operation among SAARC member States. At the Colombo Summit in 1991, and Inter-Governmental Group (IGG) was set up on the recommendation of Committee on Economic Co-operation to formulate and seek agreement on institutional framework under which specific measures for trade liberalization among SAARC member States could be pursued. Then the Inter-Governmental Group after two meetings during 1992 finalised a draft Agreement of SAARC Preferential Trading Arrangement (SAPTA) which was subsequently approved by the CEC and other bodies[21]. Finally, the Heads of State and Government of the Seven Members of SAARC signed the Agreement on SAPTA on 11 April 1993 in Dhaka during their seventh Summit. This trading arrangement came into operation from December 7, 1995, aiming at dismantling trade barriers among the member - countries and realising the goal of a South Asian Free Trade Area (SAFTA) by the year 2005 A.D. The former Indian Prime Minister Narasimha Rao, supporting strongly the idea of frontierless trade in the region at the Seventh SAARC Summit in Dhaka in 1993, where SAPTA was born, said;

"Let us break down trade barriers between us .... the one billion people of South Asia make up a mega market with the backing of positive political will, we'll become a serious player in the global economy"[22].

SAPTA may mark the first major step towards South Asia emerging as a trading zone. It would call for broader economic co-operation among member countries in the area of protection, enhancing production capacities in various economic fields and general economic growth. Setting up SAARC Chamber of Commerce would foster greater co-operation and help overcome hindrances in regional trade and co-operation. Such enhanced co-operation might herald a new atmosphere Leading to solution of political disputes such as one between India and Pakistan.

SAPTA is a contractual agreement providing a framework of rules and modalities for gradual liberalization of intra-regional trade among SAARC member States. The main aim of SAPTA is to promote and sustain mutual trade co-operation among the contracting States through exchange of concessions on their exportable/importable commodities in the form of elimination of tariff, non-tariff and para-tariff barriers[23], and direct trade measures such as long and medium terms contracts, import and supply commitments, buy, back arrangements, etc.

The basic principles governing the agreement are reciprocity and natural advantage for all member nations taking into account their respective levels of economic and industrial development, external trade, trade and tariff policies and systems and other relevant factors[24]. It is stipulated that SAPTA will be negotiated step-by-step, improved and extended in successive stages with periodic reviews. Initially negotiations will be conducted on a product-by-product basis. Another notworthy principles incorporated in the Agreement is the scope of special and preferential treatment for the Least Developed Countries. The significance of SAPTA lies in the fact that it establishes a clear possibility of full integration of SAARC economies in future[25].

The implications of the SAPTA for individual countries and what gains would be devided by each of them would be guaged only when the details of trade liberalisation are worked out. Among the seven SAARC countries - India may be perceived to be in an advantageous position. The size of India's economy, in terms of GNP, is more than three times larger than the sum total of GNP of all other six countries. India's annual export is about twice the total exports of other countries. Imports of all six coun-tries taken together are about two-thirds of India's annual import. India's hopes of deriving advantages from such a position are however, restricted, because SAPTA envisages to safeguard the interest of all member countries by stipulating that all countries would share the benefits of trade expansion equally.

Safeguard measures under SAPTA would protect the interest of comparatively weaker countries. Thus the concessions can be suspended by member countries, suffering from serious injuries to their domestic industries or from balance of payments difficulties. The least developed countries are expected to be provided special and more favourable treatment by other countries. Technical assistance and co-operation would be offered to them for establishing industrial and agricultural projects.

India having a comparatively stronger base of capital goods industries and other engineering and manufacturing industries, SAARC countries would look upon India as a preferable source of capital goods and other manufactured products, given the competitive advantage of Indian goods. In respect of agricultural items, India can hope to export larger quantities of items like tea, cotton, jute, rice, milk and milk products.

Indo-Srilanka trade and economic ties have remained intact, despite ethnic conflict in Srilanka, India can increase exports of items like railways rolling stock, machine tools, commercial vehicles, telecommunication equipment, electrical equipment, synthetic fiberes, pharmacuticals and sports goods. On a broader economic co-operation front, India has offered technical assistanace in areas like fishries, diry forming, livestock development and agro-based industries, and can help set up joint ventures in Srilanka in various fields including agro - based products, electric and electronic goods, light engineering, jewellery, textiles, leather garments, cement paper and pulp.

Indo-Bangladesh trade has remained one sided and restricted because Bangladesh has little to sell to India. Bangladesh's readiness to open its rail, road and sea corridors for trade would enhance bilateral trade. Credit offered by India to Bangladesh for industrial and infrastructural development in sectors including cement, railways, chemicals and sugar, and prospects of joint ventures in Bangladesh would lead to trade expansion. Bangladesh is particularly keen on joint ventures in milk and dairy products and textiles because their imports presently claim huge foreign exchange outgo. For harnessing abundant domestic gas supply in that country, India is willing to co-operate is setting up gas-based power and fertilizer plants.

Imports by India from Pakistan are treated at par with imports from other countries under India's import policy, Pakistan's trade policies adopt a discriminatory stand towards India. India faces difficulties in exporting several of 571 permissible items listed by Pakistan for import from India. India is in a postion to supply engineering goods to Pakistan, but the latter imports them from other countries at higher cost. However, larger two-way trade and economic co-operation would remain unexploited, notwithstanding SAPTA, so long as political relations are not normalised.

Nepal enjoys various concessions and favourable treatment in its trade with India and SAPTA would further such preferential trading facilities between the two countries. Indian companies can help Nepal is stepping up economic growth, in view of the latters liberalized measures, full convertibility of currency and free movement of goods between the two countries. India can play a major role in Nepal's quest for industrialisation through joint ventures in areas like agro-based industries, pharmacuticals, light engineering, sugar, textiles, power generation and cereal preparations.

Poverty Alleviation may be considered the main motive force behind SAPTA. As many as 47 percent of the World's poor live in the South Asian region, in terms of income levels. GNP per capita in this region ranges between US $ 180 to US $ 430. The national economies of this region are prove to massive unforseen dislocations, both natutai and manmade, which pose challenges to the task of development. Agriculture, the mainstay of the region, suffers from periodic shocks due to erratic monsoons and floods[26]. The likely expansion of trade through SAPTA may contribute to poverty alleviation by generating new employment opportunities for the ordinary people at different levels of production and export services. Moreover, the common man will have access at relatively cheaper rates to some of the commodities and consumer products which are otherwise imported from far-off developed countries at exarbitant net prices and high transportation costs[27].

The SAPTA Agreement also provides for certain additional measures. These are listed below (SAARC, 1993, Annex 1)28:

(i) the identification, preparation and establishment of industrial and agricultural projects in the territories of Least Developed member countries, which could provide the production base for the expansion of exports of these countries to other member countries, possibly linked to co-operative financing and buyback arrangements;

(ii) the setting up of manufacturing and other facilities in the least developed member countries to meet intra-regional demand under co-operative arrangements;

(iii) the formation of export promotion policies and the establishment of training facilities in the field of trade to assist the least developed countries in expanding their exports and in maximising their benefits from SAPTA;

(iv) the provision of support to export marketing of products of least developed member countries by enabling these countries to share existing facilities and by institutional and other positive measures to facilitate imports from least developed member countries into their markets;

(v) bringing together of enterprises in other member countries with project sponsors in the least developed member countries with a view to promoting joint ventures in projects designed to lead to the expansion of trade;

(vi) The provision of special facilities and rates in respect to shipping.

The measures indicated above are in addition to the special treatment for the least developed member countries as per the provisions of special treatment, the member countries are expected to provide, wherever possible, special and more favourable treatment exclusively to the least developed member countries such as[29]:

(a) duty-free access, exiusive tariff preferences or deeper-tariff preferences for the export products;

(b) the removal of non-tariff barriers;

(c) the removal where appropriate, of para-tariff barriers;

(d) special consideration of exports from least developed member countries in the application of safeguard measures;

(e) greater flexibility in the introduction and continuance of quantitative or other restrictions provisionally and without discrimination in critical circumstances by the least developed member countries on imports from other member countries.

The procedure for finalising the list of products for preferential treatment involves the exchange of lists of products for trade concessions among member countries. The SAPTA agreement provides for the establishment of a "Committee of Participants" consisting of representatives of member countries for overseeing the implementation of the Agreement. This committee is expected to meet atleast once a year to review the progress made in the implementation of the agreement and to ensure benefits of trade expansion emanating from the Agreement acute to all member countries equitably. The committee is expected to accord adequate opportunities for consultation on representations made by any member country with respect to any matter offencing the implementation of the Agreement. The committee is expected to formulate its own rules and procedures for setting representations from the member countries. Article 21 of the SAPTA Agreement provides scope for any member country to withdraw from the Agreement at any time after its coming into force[30].

## Response To Sapta By SAARC Countries

SAPTA might come into force hopefully early in 1996, the question that one would like to ask it; "what would be response to SAPTA by SAARC countries and what would be the impact of the SAPTA Agreement on the region"?

Bangladesh has signed the SAPTA with much enthusiasm[31]. Referring to the SAPTA, Prime Minister Khalida Zia termed it as an "important landmark in SAARC"[32]. The President of the Federation of Bangladesh Chambers of Commerce and Industry (FBCCI), Mahbubur Rahman said that SAPTA would create a lot of opportunities for benefitting from expansion of intra-regional trade in South Asia considering the very low share at present. He also added that the member countries of SAPTA would gain from tariff and non-tariff concenssions[33].

Bangladesh has not ratified the SAPTA, because much has not been quantified about the benefits which are expected to be reaped by it. Its dilemma of talking further step to implement SAPTA has been reflected in Bangladesh's proposal of a list of products for tariff ,concession in which Bangladesh proposed 56 items to India, 51 to Nepal and 28 to Srilanka. The list of 500 items exportable to Bangladesh proposed by India has embarrassed the Bangladesh officials. India has reduced the list by almost half and has also agreed to cut it further[34]. Most of the products on which Bangladesh has sought tariff concession are also produced in the major partner countries themselves, and hence the letter's import of these products are hardly likely to increase even if trade barriers are fully removed[35]. The narrow export base of Bangladesh is a major impediment in this regard.

Bhutan's official position on SAPTA is reflected in the statement of King of Bhutan, Jigme Singha Wangchuck, who said, "The SAPTA which seeks to expand intra-regional trade through reduction of barriers will go a long way in bringing tangible benefits to our people". He further said, "In this regard I may mention that Bhutan already enjoys to benefits of free trade with our close friend and neighbour, India"[36]. The Bhutan Chamber of Commerce and Industry has been a partner of SAARC Chamber of Commerce and Industry (SCCI) in order to carry out the activities of SAPTA in the private sector in Bhutan. Bhutan may not have worked out its due economic benefits through SAPTA which possitively may have delayed her ratification of the SAPTA.

India lending full support to SAPTA. The Indian Prime Minister, P.V. Narasimha Rao, said that India would join the collective endeavour to implement the Agreement. The Indian State Minister for External Affairs, R.L. Bhatia, said : "Our commitment to the SAPTA reflects our desire to promote the welfare of the peoples of South Asia, to improve the quality of life and to accelerate economic growth and social progress on our common objectives"[37].

SAPTA was greeted with much enthusiasm both at the government and non-government levels in India, New Delhi has not yet ratified it. The cause of her unwillingness to ratify SAPTA is the selective commodity-by-commodity negotiation for progressive tariff reduction provided under SAPTA is going to be a slow, long-drawn-out process. Besides, political considerations may lead any of the seven member states to stall the whole process. On the part of India, an alternative approach which will be quite viable and feasible in integration of the market of India separately with the markets of those South Asian countries which are prepared to travel along this route[38].

The Maldives also supports SAPTA, but with some qualification. Mr. Fatullah Jameel, Foreign Minister of Maldives, has given the rationale of the Maldives support for SAPTA, as he stated, "we will not benefit much from SAPTA, but we are looking to the interest of the people of the region"[39]. Such a perception may have prevented the Maldives from ratifying the SAPTA Agreement. The Maldivian business community also stands for SAPTA with their government. The Maldivian

Trader's Association has become a member of SAARC Chamber of Commerce and Industries.

Nepal has been positive about SAPTA. The Nepalese Former Minister for Tourism and Civil Aviation, Ram Hari Joshi, has opined that the successful implementation of the SAPTA and the Plan of Action for eradicating poverty would usher in new and promising era for effective region co-operation in South Asia[40]. Nepal strongly endorses SAPTA because over 30 percent of the total volume of Nepales foreign trade is with SAARC member states which could increase when SAPTA would become a reality[41]. Nepal has also started implementing it by allowing to percent tariff concessions to all goods imparted from SAARC countries. The Federation of Nepal Chambers of Commerce and Industry (FNCCI) is a constituent body of SCCI. The FNCCI viewed as a step towards poverty alleviation, as the people can get less-costly items from around the region.

Pakistan has took a negative approach to the proposal of SAPTA, in the beginning. But afterwards, Pakistan signed the SAPTA agreement due to the consesus that without an agreement on trade there is little possibility of pushing the SAARC process forward[42]. Prime Minister of Pakistan, Nawaz Sharif said, "The SAPTA arrangement will stimulate our economies through co-operation in a regional contex"[43].

The favourable attitude of Pakistan seemed to have hastend the implementation process of SAPTA, Pakistan's position still remains uncertain. Its doubtfulness has been projected in Bangladesh-Pakistan economic relations. While Bangladesh highlights the importance of trade relations at the regional level and emphasizes on the removal of trade barriers, Pakistan continues to focus on the bilateral trade. This is evident in the statement of V.A. Jaffrey, the Adviser to the Prime Minister of Pakistan Benazir Bhutto on Financial and Economic Affairs, who said that trade "is not possible in the basket of SAPTA as there are not only economic problems, but also political disputes within the region"[44]. Pakistan's hesitation is caused by its hostile relations with India and its fear of India's giant industrial base which may be a threat to Pakistan's industry and trade. India's emphasis on trade co-operation bilaterally rather than multilaterally has added a further note of doubt for Pakistan. Pakistan expressed itsdesire to make major reductions of tariffs at rates higher than those it planned for members of ECO (Economic Co-operation Organization). Besides government's guarded optimism about SAPTA, the Pakistani business community seems to be enticed by the prospects of the regional market for their products.

Srilanka was the initiator of the proposal of SAPTA. In the opinion of Srilankan former Foreign Minister, A.C.S. Hameed, it was imperative for all SAARC member countries to extend their fullest co-operation to ensure the share of benefits of trade expansion equitably. This would enhance the negotiating capacity of SAARC with other trading blocs. He also assured that his country would extend its fullest co-operation to make SAPTA operational by the end of 1995[45].

The business community of Srilanka is enthusiastic about the implementation of SAPTA. They envisage that SAPTA would place South Asia at par with the rest of the world[46]. The Federation of Chambers of Commerce and Industry of Srilanka is a member of SAARC Chamber of Commerce and Industry. From the above review, a common point appears that all the members of SAARC are committed to trade co-operation through SAPTA. The overarching presence of India, in terms of its giant economic size, generates fear in the smaller economies of SAARC and poses a major threat to the successful trade co-operation by means of SAPTA. But the underdevelopment of the South Asian States and the ongoing global trend of trade co-operation render the need for the expansion of trade through SAPTA an imperative.

Various moves have been made by SAARC member countries to achieve the goal of South Asian free trade Area (SAFTA)[47]:

(a) proposal have been made for a single currency a regional bank, financial institutions, a SAARC stock Exchange and a SAARC corporate club;

(b) the inter-governmental trade and economic co-operation is complemented by the business community from the SAARC member countries through the apex body, that is, the SAARC chamber of Commerce and Industry (SCCI) with its headquarters at Karachi;

c) with the theme "co-operation for growth", the first SAARC fair was held at New Delhi from January 9-14, 1996, with the aim of improving trade relations among member-countries;

(d) the member-countries of the SAARC have given the mandate to an Inter-Governmental Group (IGG) of offi-cials to negotiate for the dismantling of trade barriers and expanding the preferential tariff coverage to the maximum possible extent under SAPTA.

The SAARC member countries have agreed to offer tariff concessions on as many as 226 items India has offered concessions on more than 1000 items to SAARC members so as to accelerate the pace of establishing SAPTA. A recent study by the International Food Policy Research Institute (IFPRI) in Washington DC estimates that intra-regional trade will expand by more than \$ 800 million following the establishment of SAPTA - which is more than double the current levels. Indian exports to the rest of the bloc are also expected to double, increasing by almost \$ 270 million. Economic welfare in that case is expected to improve by \$ 5,588 million per year - more than 25 items the level estimated under SAPTA. At present, the SAPTA countries in general and India in particular, are in consequential feather weights when it comes to global trade[48].

As second round of negotiation, under SAPTA-II as many as 2013 products have been offered concessions of which 764 have been exclusively in favour of least developed countries.

India has offered the maximum number of concessions numbering 911 products (favouring mainly Bangladesh), followed by Pakistan - 386 products. In return, India has received concessions in respect of 474 products. The largest number of concessions have been in favour of Bangladesh (600 products), followed by Pakistan (646 products). It will be seen that India and Nepal have not exchanged any concessions under SAPTA-II since they have earlier exchanged deeper concessions under a bilateral trade agreement[49].

In a prior study based on data for 1994-95 it nas been established that in order to liberalise nearly the total bilateral trade with its neighbours, India needs merely to liberalize its to fifty products imported from these countries[50].

A notable feature of the second round of negotiations is that unlike the negotiations under the first round, the non-tariff measures applicable on imports have been specified (mainly by India, being perhaps the only country having such a wide coverage of non-tariff measures). Further, India has relaxed such measures in favour of least developed countries[51].

The SAPTA Committee of participants established under Article 9 of the Agreement of SAARC Preferential Trading Arrangement (SAPTA), reviewed progress in the implementation of the SAPTA Agreement and finalised the Draft Rules of Procedure of the Committee. This was the first meeting of the committee held at the SAARC Secretariat, Kathmandu on 25-26 February, 1997[52].

The committee felt that wider publicity be given to the national schedules of concessions among the business community in each contracting state to enable it to derive maximum benefit under SAPTA Agreement. The Committee held in-depth deliberations on the uniform format of certificate of origin. It was agreed that Bangladesh has prepare a sample certificate of origin with the agreed specifications and circulate the same to the contracting states by end of March 1997. It was also agreed that the uniform certificate of origin would be adopted in all the scontracting states by end of June 1997. All countries would than supply country-wise data about imports from other SAARC Countries under SAPTA and outside SAPTA as per approved formats. The future meetings of the committee would be held by rotation in contracting state in alphabetical order[53].

The success of SAPTA is likely to be impeded by two types of obstacles, political and economic. These two sets of factors are interwoven and mutually reinforcing. Political obstacles emerge from the inter-state relations in South Asia which are characterized by tae existence of a number of long-standing bilateral disputes. Economic obstacles are a combination of weak industrial base, fragile infrastructure, lack of capital etc., which are affecting the individual, states of South Asia, thereby, hindering regional economic development[54].

Long-term benefits may be achieved by SAPTA in many areas. Its potentials remain for exploration of natural resources, human capital formation, exploitation of dynamic gains from trade through maximizing various linkages and economies of scale, technological spurt and appropriate technological innovations. Productive efficiency originating from managerial efficiencies on the basis of comparative advantage and augmenting efficiencies emanating from competition which act as catalyst elements in the development process of the region. Beyond these factors, the more SAPTA will be taking its institutional shape, the more will it strengthen the bargaining capacity of SAARC countries with the developed West. The emergence of SAPTA lies in the need for eradicating object poverty of the South Asian countries as well as the external fear of maginalization arising out of the ongoing global trend of regional economic co-operation. However, the South Asian countries have accepted the reality of trade co-operation through SAPTA with India at the heart of the region. The strengthening of SAPTA in South Asia depends upon India's gesture with regard to its concessions about the implementation of SAPTA[55].

It may be emphasised that, even after SAPTA is fully implemented and other ongoing efforts for promoting economic co-operation have yielded results South Asia will still remain far from having a single market[56].

## An Appraisal

While listing the achievement and prospects of SAARC, mention must also be made of a number of measures initiated by it to promote increased linkages with non-governmental voluntary organizations in order to promote greater people-to-people contact and increased involvement of the peoples of South Asia in the process of regional co-operation. In the context the formulation of guidelines and procedures for extending recognition to regional apex bodies has facilitated their participation in promoting regional co-operation at the people-to-people level SAARC is also concerned with establishing in inhancing its linkages with other regional organizations. Contacts between recognised regional apex bodies of SAARC and ASEAN are being encouraged, and the identification of the mutually beneficial areas of co-operation in proposed to be done on a priority basis.

Not only this, the success of the SAARC outside its stated areas of activity has indeed been remarkable. The occasions of interaction and exchange of views provided during the SAARC meetings have been positively used by the SAARC leaders to sort out a number of bilateral issues with their neighbourhood colleagues. As such, not only possible crises have been avoided but conflictual issues have been dealt with to seek their final resolution which, in turn, has facilitated mutual understanding and rapport. India-Srilanka and India-Pakistan talks during the SAARC Summits and Ministerial meeting during 1985, 1986, 1987, 1988 and 1997-1998, may be recalled here. The conclusion of three Indo-Pakistan agreements, including one on non-attack on each others nuclear facilities, during the Islamabad Summit, may be treated as the high watermark of success of the SAARC in the field of mutual confidence-building in the region.

The Programming Committee considered proposals for the establishment of regional institutions in various areas of co-operation under the Integrated Programme of Action in there meeting held in 11-12 November 1986 at Bangalore, India. It reviewed the status of the proposals setting up of SAARC Mateorological Research Centre (SMRC), SAARC Agricultural Information Centre (SALC), Regional Software Centre for Telecommunications, Regional Tuberculosis Centre, Institute of Transport Technology and Training, Regional Centre for Postal Research and Development, Design Centre for Floating Craft, Shipping Conference of SAARC countries, SAARC shipping Council, and Regional Institute for Appropriate Rural Technology.

The two days meeting of the Government Council of the South Asian Co-operative Environment Programme (SACEP) began in Colombo, September 21, 1992, with a discussion on setting up a South Asian Co-operative Environment Programme Trust Fund.

The SAARC framework has taken measures to promote co-operation in social, cultural, scientific and economic fields. These programmes are : The SAARC Audio visual Exchange (SAVE) programmes SAARC Education Exchange Programmes, SAARC chairs, fellowships and scholarships scheme SAARC Youth Volunteer Programme, SAARC SCheme for promotion of organized tourism, SAARC visa exemption scheme and programmes for co-operation among Non-Governmental organi-zations. The SAARC as a regional body has taken initiatives to promote co-operation with inter-regional organizations. A memorandum of understanding signed between SAARC and UNCTAD provides SAARC updated versions of the software, viz., Trade Analysis and Information Systems (Trains) which a computerised information system containing latest information on trade control measures prevailing in fifty developed and developing countries of the world. The SAARC Secretariat would provide similar information about trade control measures of SAARC member countries to the UNCTAD. This arrangement would help all the SAARC Countries[57].

The SAARC Secretariat has signed a co-operation agreement with the United Nations Children's Fund (UNICEF) to implement the programmes envisaged by SAARC as well as for carrying out studies to monitor the implementation. Similar agreements of co-operation have been signed with the Economic and Social Commission for Asia and Pacific (ESCAP), International Telecommunication Union (ITU) and the Asia Pacific Telecommunity.

The SAARC member countries have signed a number of conventions and agreements in different areas indicated as : Agreement on Establishing the SAARC Food Security Reserve (Nov. 1987), SAARC Regional Convention on Suppression of Terrorism (Nov. 1987) and SAARC convention on Narcotic Drugs and Psychotropic Sustances (Nov. 1990), etc.[58] The SAARC has also carried out a number of studies and brought out reports. The area coverd by SAARC reports includes "Women in Development", "Trade, Manufactures and Services", "Disasters and environment", "Green House effect", and "Poverty alleviation".

Creating adequate political will among the SAARC leadership and public is required to improve free trade, industrial and economic co-operation in an era of globalisation and liberalisation. Removal of discriminatory trade practices among member countries should be the first step. Secondly, macro-economic reforms aimed at higher growth and greater economic resilience, must be extended and deepened. Thirdly collective negotiating mechanism in dealing with multinational institution is called for. For instance, some trade is routed through non-SAARC coun-tries to by-pass restrictions. It should be removed, and the coverage of intra-SAARC trade should be promoted, by encouraging multinationals and by establishing joint ventures in the SAARC countries. India may take initiative in this regard; establishing joint ventures in Nepal, Srilanka, Bangladesh, Pakistan, Bhutan and Maldives.

Similarly, these SAARC countries can sell primary products and manufactured goods to India and other member countries. For example, Bhutan is currently providing India with electricity from Chukha Hydel Project, a major source of export revenue. Bilateralism should be strengthened to improve and normalise political relations. Fourthly, natural resources must be managed so that the region's development path is environmentally sustainable. Fifthly, bilateralism should be strengthened to improve and normalise political relations. Since the SAARC charter makes room for other members to join the association, it will be no doubt a helpful exercise if efforts are made and particularly though Indian initiatives to make Myanmar (Burma) Thailand, Afghanistan and Iran to join this forum. Iran and Myanmar have already expressed their willingness to become members of SAARC grouping. It is hoped that with the passage of time, SAARC nations will be able to harmonise their views on economic issues, so that they can exert greater influence in relevant international fora as a group[59].

At the invitation of the World Tourism Organization (WTO) and the Government of the Maldives, Secretary-General, Naeem U. Hasan attended the Asia-Pacific Ministerial Conference on Tourism and Environment held in Male from February 15 to 17, 1997. The Secretary General was accompanied by Director Ahmed Latheef[60].

With the fruitful outcome of the meeting in Male, Secretary General headed towards Tokyo for consultations with the Japanese Government on the Working of the SAARC Japan Special Fund with a view to improving the effectiveness and expansion of the activities under the fund. This was followed by a visit to Beijing by the Secretary Genral at the invitation of the Chinese Government for talks on the proposed Seminar on SAARC-China co-operation to be held in Chinese capital in 1997[61].

Thus, if one were to sum up SAARC achievements till to day, one can do so only in a relative sense. Taking note of serious bilateral differences among member states, the achilvements though modest, appear to be of some significance considering that the foundations for increased regional co-operation are being laid. Enhancing the possibilities of greater people-to-people contract (for which steps have been initiated) would further hasten this process. The point that needs to be grasped in the South Asian context is that there is a mutually reinforcing positive relationship between the bilateral and the regional affairs and easing of bilateral concerns and warries will go a long way in advancing regional understanding and co-operation. The regional political context is changing for the better. The positive turn in India-Srilanka relations following the conclusion of an agreement between the two countries in July 1987 on the issue of Srilanka's ethnic problem, is there for any one to see. This has not only brought about strategic convergence between the two countries, but also heralded a new era of enhanced economic co-operation between them. A similar convergence has also come to be established between India and the Maldives following the former's decisive role in frustrating the coup attempt against the. Gayoom regime against the background of the'se positive developments, one hopefully looks forward to the growth and consolidation of mutual trust and understanding among the member states paving way for a truely catalytic role of the SAARC in heralding a new era of growth and prosperity in South Asia.

## References

1. Jagdish Lal, 'Third Concepts'; An International Journal of Ideas; December 1993, p. 26.
2. P.K. Mishra, South-South Co-operation and SAARC; Monthly Public Openion Survey, 34 (10-11), July/Aug. 1989; p. 15.
3. S.N. Raghavan, "Regional Economic Co-operation among

SAARC Countries"; Sponsored by Economic and Scientific Research Foundation, New Delhi and Friedrich Naumann Foundation, New Delhi; p. 15.

4. P.K. Mishra, South-South Co-operation and SAARC; Monthly Public Opinion Survey, 34 (10-11), Jul/Aug. 1989, p.15.
5. 'News Letter', News from South Asian Association for Regional co-operation; Published by SAARC Secretariat, Kathmandu, Nepal.
6. Mainstream, Vol. XXXV, No. 7, January 25, 1997; pp. 47-50.
7. Mollica Dastidar, "SAARC Decade Action Plan for the Girl Child (1991-2000); Mainstream, Vol. 31, March 6, 1993; pp. 25-26.
8. V. Kanesalingam, 'General Overview of SAARC's Achievements; MARGA Quarterly Journal, Vol. 12, No. 1, 1991, Published by MARGA INSTITUTE (Srilanka Centre for Development Studies); p. 13.
9. Jagdish Lal, Third Concept; An International Journal of Ideas, December 1993, p. 26.
10. Preamble of the convention. Hereinafter reference is made to Articles of the SAARC Regional Convention on Suppression of Terrorism, Signed at Kathmandu, Nepal on November 4, 1987.
11. Mizanur Rehman, BIISS Journal, Vol. 9, No.2, 1988, pp. 271-276.
12. Jagdish Lal, Third Concept; An International Journal of Ideas, December 1993, p. 26.
13. S.N. Raghavan, "Regional Economic Co-operation among SAARC Countries", sponsored by Economic and Scientific Research Foundation, New Delhi and Friedrich Naumann Foundation, New Delhi, p. 18.
14. Rehman Sobham, "The Logic of Placing Economic Co-operation on the SAARC Agenda", in Imtiaz Ahmed and Meghna Guhathaputra (eds.), SAARC: Beyond State-Centric Co-operation, Centre for Social Studies (CSS), Dhaka, 1992,

p. 40.

15. Sabbir Ahmed "SAARC Preferential Trading Arrangement: A Preliminary Analysis"; BIISS Journal, Vol. No.2, 1995, p. 165.

16. Regional Studies, Vol. XVI, No. 1, WINTER 1997-98, p. 98.

17. S.N. Raghavan, 'Regional economic co-operation among SAARC Countries', sponsord by Economic and Scientific Research Foundation, New Delhi and Friedrich Neumann Foundation, New Delhi, p. 18.

18. Indra Nath Mukherji, "SAARC: Its Economic Achievements"; World Focus, Monthly Discussion Journal, Vol. 14, no.7, July 1993, p. 10.

19. Regional Studies, Vol. XVI, No. 1, WINTER 1997-98, pp.98-99.

20. Manoranjan Mohanty, "Borderless SAARC Region : A Distant Dream"?; Mainstream, Vol. XXXV, No. 26, June 7, 1997, p. 12.

21. Sabbir Ahmed, "SAARC Preferential Trading Arrangement: A Preliminary Analysis"; BIISS Journal, Vol. 16, No.2, 1995, p. 166.

22. S. Mustafa (1993), "SAPTA steps out", Dhaka Courier, Dhaka, March 16, p. 7.

23. Sabbir Ahmed, "SAARC Preferential Trading Arrangement: A Preliminary Analysis", BIISS Journal, Vol. 16, No.2, 1995, p. 166.

24. Kamal Hossain, "SAARC 2000 and Beyond", p. 117.

25. See, the original document of Agreement on SAARC Preferential Trading Arrangement (SAPTA).

26. Inaugural speech by the President of SAARC Chambers of Commerce and Industry, Souvenir, Dhaka, 7 February 1994.

27. Mr. R.M. Roy, "SAARC Preferential Trading Arrangement (SAPTA).", paper presented at the national seminar on SAARC Preferential Trading Arrangement (SAPTA), jointly organised by the Federation of Bangladesh Chambers of

Commerce and Industry and Friedrich-Naumann-Stiftung (FNSt), Dhaka, 24 July 1994.

28. S.N. Raghavan, "Regional Economic Co-operation among SAARC Countries", pp. 104-122.
29. Ibid.
30. Ibid.
31. Sabbir Ahmed, "SAARC Preferential Trading Arrangement, A Preliminary Analysis", BIISS Journal, Vol. 16, no.2, 1995, pp. 165-196.
32. The Bangladesh Observer, Dhaka, 12 April 1993.
33. The Financial Express, Dhaka, 25 July 1994.
34. Dhaka Courier, Dhaka, 10 December 1993, p. 5.
35. Ayubur Rahman Bhuyan, op. cit., p. 9.
36. Kuensel, Bhutan's National Newspaper, 17 April 1993.
37. The Statesman, Calcutta, 11 April 1993.
38. Muchkund Dubey, "Indo-Bangladesh Economic Relations", Seminar paper presented at the International Seminar on "Society, Polity and Economy of Bangladesh", organised by the Centre for South, Central, Southeast Asian and Southwest Pacific Studies, School of International Studies, J.N.U., New Delhi, 7-8 March 1994, p. 21.
39. The Financial Express, Dhaka, 4 December 1993.
40. The Bangladesh Observer, Dhaka, 25 May 1994.
41. The Independent, Kathmandu, 13 April 1994.
42. Rashid Ahmad Khan, op. cit. p. 51.
43. Dawn, Karachi, 9 April, 1993.
44. The Financial Express, Dhaka, 14 July 1994.
45. The Bangladesh Observer, Dhaka, 5 December 1993.
46. Daily News, Colombo, 4 August 1994.
47. Manoranjan Mohanty, "Borderless SAARC Region : A Distant Dream"?; Mainstream, Vol. XXXV, No. 26, June 7, 1997.

48. Dr. Vijay Shukla, "New Frontiers of SAARC", Mishra, Pramod Kumar (ed.), 'Dhaka to New Delhi: one decade of SAARC; India Quarterly, 52(1-2), June 96; p. 92.
49. I.N. Mukherji, "Healing the Wound - Prospects of SAPTA", Mainstream, Vol. 35, May 17, pp. 13-15.
50. Paper on "Guidelines for India's offer and Request list in the Second Round of Negotiations", presented at the SAARC Brainstorming Session (Workshop), Research and Information System for Non-Aligned and other Deve-loping Countries, New Delhi, Sept. 17-18, 1996 (being part of the results of a research project sponsored by the International Development Research Institute, Ottawa, Cananda).
51. Ibid.
52. 'News Letter', News from the South Asian Association for Regional co-operation; published by SAARC Secretariat, Kathmandu, Nepal.
53. Ibid.
54. Sabbir Ahmed, "SAARC Preferential Trading Agrangement: A Preliminary Analysis;" BIISS Journal, Vol. 16, No.2, 1995, p. 190.
55. Ibid, p. 196.
56. Kamal Hossain, "SAARC 2000 and Beyond", p. 118.
57. S.N. Raghavan, "Regional Economic Co-operation among SAARC Countries", Sponsord by Economic and Scientific Research Foundation, New Delhi and Friedrich Naumann Foundation, New Delhi, p. 16.
58. Ibid.
59. Dr. Vijay Shukla, "New Frontiers of SAARC", Mishra, Pramod Kumar (ed.), 'Dhaka to New Delhi: one decade of SAARC'; India Quarterly, 52 (1-2), June 96, p. 92.
60. 'News Letter', News from South Asian Association for Regional Co-operation; Published by SAARC Secretariat, Kathmandu, Nepal.
61. Ibid.

# 6

# Conclusion

South Asia with its all defined external boundries, constitute a coherent region, there is very little linkage among the states a legacy of colonial rule. After the British withdrawal some of the states developed close links with external powers rather than among themselves. Due to mutual threat perception, the regional states have invited the external powers to play a major security role. Fear of India made Pakistan give a security role to the U.S. Fear of U.S., China and Pakistan acting together against India made India yield a security role to the Soviet Union[1]. These external alignments work powerfully to sustain the very conditions that define the insecurity of regional states. They may make available the power resources to the Regional States but are unable to control or mitigate the sources of tensions that make the State insecure. This is mainly because it is not derived from the internal dynamics of a particular region, but is only an attempt externally.

In this blurred security secenario, two options appears available by which the Regional States can enhance their security. One is through non-alignment and the other through regional co-operation. The birth of South Asian Association for Regional Co-operation (SAARC) in December 1985 at Dhaka is viewed as an optioning of a new chapter in South

Asian history[2]. This is very fact that SAARC was established at all was a positive development, for the agreement of the seven countries of South Asia to the Bangladeshi proposal for a Regional Organization Committed them to work together for the progress and well-being of one fifth of humanity that calls South Asia its home[3]. The SAARC no doubt has considerable potential for the ground for a common approach to security in the region. It has members, big and small, opened strong up opportunities evolving problems for its and weak, to achieve that they so far could not, "to promote and strength collective self-reliance and to contribute to mutual trust, understanding and appreciation of one another's problems"[4]. SAARC has generated certain hopes for the future of South Asian Security.

Having agreed jointly on a charter and on common goals, the member countries cannot afford to be indifferent to them, or to show a lack of will be co-operate on account or their differing perceptions. As they play host to SAARC meetings at various levels in rotation, their leaders are virtually under compulsion to articulate and uphold the idealistic purposes of the organization. This factor operates as a contraint on the more powerful member, and India in particular, in their pursuit of National Interests or Hegemonic Ambitions[5]. The emergence of SAARC in this context has been viewed with a mix of some optimism and lot of scepticism. Optimism, because for the first time here is a forum wherein the States have the opportunity for closer interaction, albiet in limited fields. Scepticism, because in the backdrop of the distorted Inter-State Relations very few observers tend to see much prospects of positive outcome of SAARC. scepticism also emerges from the fact that SAARC has for the present adopted what has been referred to as a Functional Approach whereby the Association has confined its Agenda to some specific socio-economic and rather non-controversial areas. The reason for adopting such an approach has also been explained in terms of the limitations to what can be expected of Regional Co-operation in the backdrop of the deep-seated problems in Inter-State Relations[6].

Whatever may be the ultimate shape of the SAARC and the pattern of its co-operative programmes, the fact remains that potential for regional co-operation in South Asia in enormous. It is possible to perceive this new forum as an avenue for greater interaction of the States at the official and people's level whereby a psycho-social environment may be created leading to greater co-operation in the future and ultimately to a peaceful and state Regional Environment. Given the political will and commitment to purpose the process of co-operation tenaciously, the SAARC process may in the future, although indirectly, turn out be a useful mechanism for tension-diffusing and mutual confidence-building, whereby the needs and imperatives for Extra-Regional Linkage would gradually erode[7].

The Technical Committees and Working Groups that have been meeting to discuss the agreed areas of co-operation have achieved concrete results which may be modest but which have contribution to development. The personal Association and interaction between the experts in these fields has been specially useful and has also served to foster a Regional Consciousness[8].

The apparent indications of SAARC's progress to be positive. The first Foreign Secretary level meeting held in April 1981 in Colombo decided to include only five areas of co-operation, namely, agriculture, rural development, communication, meteorology, health and population. The number of the areas included in the Integrated Programme of Action (IPA) has since grown considerably and now covers; sports, arts, culture, postal services, tourism, transport, education, scientific and technological collaboration, women and child development, suppression of terrorism, control of drug abuse, environment, disaster management, food security, audio-visual exchanges and planning experiences, etc. Many SAARC fellowships and chairs have been established. A consensus has been reached on the definition of terrorism and a convention on steps tot its prevention has been signed. A common stand to be adopted on North-South Issues has been agreed upon. A decision has been taken to build up a reserve stock of food grains in every member country for Regional Food Security System. Agreement has also been arrived at to foster people to people contact among the countries of the region by providing fillip to regional tourism and general promotion of co-operation in the field of art and culture[9]. The broadcasting of programmes of music and folk dances of various countries by Radio and Television in all member States, and the staging of South Asian Games have already become established as popular features of co-operation between them.

The extention of regional co-operation to core areas of trade, industry, energy and finance may have a substantial impact on the economic prospects of SAARC countries. Only the liberalization of interregional trade by establishing Preferential Trading Arrangments will facilitat the development of an Economic Community in the South Asian Region. All States in the region are tied to dependency linkages with the Industrial States for aid, trade, and technology[10]. There is an immediate need to establish high degree of mutual confidence in the unity of Regional Economic co-operation before integrating with the North and within the South co-operation framework. The reason of mistrust is that the smaller states of SAARC fear that the freeing of regional trade would only facilitate India's Domination of their economies[11].

The Industrial Development Plants in South Asia have so long aimed at establishing import-sustaining indus-tries. Preferences for such policies will be guided by poor Foreign Exchange earnings. This has produced duplication of industrial process in South Asia. These efforts epitomized by the catchy slogans of self-reliance have not only led to protectionist policies, but have also created a class of economically influential people whose vested interests do not allow liberal trade flows in the South Asian Region. The large sizse of the South Asian Consumer Market - which comprises one fourth of the human population - requires that future economic and industrial planning of the SAARC members rest on a rational division of labour on the basis of factor endowment and comparative advantage. A common trade policy in raw materials and a unified bargaining position on commodity exports must be developed through the SAARC forum for neutralizing the adverse impact of shifts in the International Commodity Market. Nevertheless, the geographical proximity and availability of relatively developed transport systems in South Asia provide the physical infra-structure for the facilitation of rapid and cost effective trade transportation[12]. The geographical factors can also be utilized for joint resource development programmes.

The development of regional economic co-operation in the SAARC region can progress rapidly if all the member, countries perceive this process as a means to accelerate economic growth in individual member countries. The main instrument for achieving regional economic co-operation is to agree on certain common programme of industrial restructuring in line with the developments taking place in other parts of the world. Secondly, it has to be ensured that the process of Regional co-operation leads to more accelerated economic growth in the relatively less developed and small member countries in the region. Thirdly, the industrial and trade policies of the member countries should facilitate expansion of intra-regional trade and investment. Fourthly, since governments by their very nature tend to take a short-term view and also tend to delay in taking decisions on many economic issues, the Private Sector should take greater initiatives in promoting Regional Economic Co-operation. It is, however, significant to note that the spectrum of possibilities for the private enterpreneum have also now widened with the process of deregulation and economic reforms progressing rapidly in all the countries in the SAARC region. This process has opened immense opportunities for the private enterpreneurs to expand trade and Commercial relations among the member countries. The process of decision-making, either for establishing Joint Ventures or making investment through transfer of technology or for expanding trade and Commerce, has become much easier now and this should be of great help in forging closer economic linkages among the

SAARC countries. To realise this potential, the SAARC Chamber of Commerce and Industry as well as the Federation of Chembers of Commerce and Industry in the member countries have to play an active role.

One important area in which the Federations could play an active role is in influencing the decisions of the Governments in respect of tariff reductions envisaged under SAPTA agreement. The SAARC Chamber in consultation with the National Federations should put forward proposals directly to the SAARC Secretariat identifying more commodities and to extent of tariff reduction that could be considered necessary for expanding intra-regional trade. Similarly, proposals have also to be made to implement tariff reduction under fast track for a list of commodities mutually agreed upon by the National Federation[13].

Most of the SAARC countries have already initiated several measures for reforming the Financial Sector. The National Federations should inform the SAARC Chamber about the policy changes introduced in the financial sector from time to time and the SAARC Chamber has to disseminate these changes to all the member countries. The National Federations should also urge the Public Sector and Private Sector Banks to expand the Branch Network to other member countries to facilitate business and commercial transactions[14].

Another related area is the operations of Stock Markets in member countries. The National Federations should supply information on a regular basis to the SAARC Chamber about the performance of Stock Markets in their own countries. The SAARC Chamber has to provide his information to other National Federations. This would help the enterpreneurs in the member countries in knowing about the performance of various industries which would facilitate in taking decisions about establishing Joint Ventures in specific branches of manufacturing activities. The SAARC Chamber has also to prepare a strategy for meeting the challenges arising out of the Uruguay Round of trade negotiations.

Dumping is another area where the SAARC Chamber and the National Federations have to work closely in collecting the necessary information for taking appropriate action. Dumping is a phenomenon which is not clearly understood by both the policy makers and the business people in the SAARC countries. The SAARC Chamber and the National Federations should establish an information system which could provide details of cost of production of different products on a regular basis.

The textiles and clothing segment, which accounts for a significant share of the exports of SAARC countries, is another area where the prospects appear to be bright after the introduction of the new GATT proposals. In the new emerging situation, the SAARC countries have to first establish their technical competence and secondly adopt sophisticated marketing strategies. The member countries have to develop their competitive advantages in particular lines of production. It is here that the countries have to co-operate modernising the production facilities like spinning, weaving of special fabrics and garment marketing. The countries have to establish strong production linkages among themselves with a view to retaining their existing market shares as well as penetrate into new markets in Global Textile Trade[15].

Co-operation among SAARC countries in the area of Research and Development (R & D) in industrial fields as well as in Agricultural Research can play an important role. For example, under the aegis of the Asian Vegetable Research and Development Centre (AVRDC), Taiwan, a network known as the South Asian Vegetable Research Network (AVER-NET) consisting of Bangladesh, Bhutan, India, Nepal, Pakistan and Srilanka has been set up. Furthermore, entomologists from the participant countries are also engaged in developing Biological Control Methods for pests and SAVERNET provided funds to improve infrastructure to rear bio-control measures in all the six SAARC countries.

The proper institutional framework is created for enabling

the scientists in different areas in all the SAARC countries to meet frequently and exchange ideas and information. Since most of the Research and development establishments in the SAARC countries are publicly funded institutions, the Governments have to take initiative to facilitate such exchange of ideas and information.

Regional co-operation under SAARC has to extend to many other areas such as banking and financial services, trading and marketing services, consultancy services as well as development of human resources through upgradation of technological and management skills. The SAARC Chamber of Commerce and Industry has proposed to appoint a number of Task Forces on many of the specific aspects indicated in this study. These task forces come up with concrete proposals that could be implemented by both the policy makers and the private sector. It is must be reiterated that the SAARC countries should prepare themselves to take advantage of the fast developments in the Global Economy[16].

Other area for innovation action to strenghen SAARC would be promote people-to-people contacts. The establishment, in October 1991, of SAARC Law, an Association of Lawyers and Jurists of the South Asian Countries, constitutes the kind of step that can help bring the people of the region together. Recent developments, have created both alarm and despondency about the future of SAARC. However as a foregoing analysis has sought to highlight, the concept of Regional co-operation has demonstrated both its relevance and efficacy, and needs to be implemented in South Asia as a major instrument of promoting economic development and eliminating poverty[17].

Another area with enormous practical potential is that of technology whose introduction in various segments of the economy and adaptation to the region's requirements can revolutionise the economic development of South Asia. Apart from the specific areas of water Resources and Energy that have already been convered, there is scope to generate self-reliance by pooling Research and Development facilities, and to build up technical expertise in the design and manufacture of engineering equipment. Regional Information Centre could also be established. Though India enjoys an enormous advantage through its progress in training technical manpower and developing sophisticated equipment, this area presently stands assigned to Pakistan which also chairs the Committee on Science and Technology (COMSTECH) of the Organization of Islamic Conference[18].

Another vital area of future Regional co-operation is Energy. Currently, per capita levels of energy consumption in South Asian Countries are among the lowest in the world.

Complementarities exist in that some countries are surplus in certain fields of energy while some have a potential surplus in others. India is rich in coal, Pakistan and Bangladesh in natural gas, while the Himalayan States have an excess of hydroelectric potential, some of the areas for Regional co-operation could be petroleum exploration, substitution of petroleum by coal, power generation, micro-hydel projects, bio-gas production and the development of wind and solar energy[19]. However, the degree of mutual trust and goodwill required to make multilateral planning of energy use possible has yet to be achieved.

A regional perspective on the sharing of River Waters may also into account the question of a judicious harnessing of the irrigation potential of these Rivers. Irrigation along with new Agricultural Techniques and Methods, particularly in the field of food-grain production, constitute vital areas for present and future needs. In South Asia, countries like India and Pakistan have made significant advances in food production and yet the prospects of food availability after depend upon unpredicable weather conditions. The existing and prospective food deficiencies in South Asia call for urgent steps towards building a Regional Food Security Programme[20].

The exploitation of sea-bed resources of India, Srilanka, Bangladesh, Pakistan and Maldives is another area where wider co-operation in the region is possible and desirable. Bilateral agreements have also been concluded between India and Srilanka and India and Bangladesh for joint scientific exploration of the sea-resources. The fact that India is aspiring to be self-sufficient in oil by 1990 on the basis of new oil wells found in the sea-bed may inspire and encourage the other South Asian countries to develop a Regional Approach in this field.

The scope for Regional Co-operation is no less promissing in the field of socio-cultural activities. A Study Group has been appointed for this with India as the co-ordination and the first meeting of group is likely to take place in Delhi by the end of June 1983. Specific subjects like films, cultural exchanges Regional games and sports, co-ordination in fine arts, literature, handicrafts etc. were indicated by India and Bangladesh in their initial working papers[21]. Co-operation in these areas would enliven the basic reality of common cultural dormant in the intra-regional interactions. Development of transport, telecommunication, and tourism in the region will give further impetus to cultural exchanges of individuals and ideas.

The Regional interaction in the field of education and scientific research is indeed very vast. Besides encouraging regional seminars and symposia, collective programmes of research and higher studies may be initiated which among other things may include setting up of educational institutions like South Asian Regional University or Centre of Asian studies in history, arts, culture, language etc. Many possibilities for training in the field of science and technology may also be worked out[22]. In view of these facts, the countries in the area can co-operate in establishing institutions of higher learning for imparting technical training for manning projects conceived for the economic development of the region.

The countries may set up appropriate agencies to secure better terms of trade from the rest of the world in the marketing of Tea, Coffee, Species, Jute and Jute goods, Hides and Skins, Fish, Fruits, Betal leaves, Chillies, Tamarind, Handicrafts and Handloom cloth, to begin with. Setting up of this agency like the International Trade Secretariat, will create interest for all the countries because they have one or the other commodities to sell to the world and benefit from the joint efforts[23].

In strengthening SAARC and making it more effective, the most important role has to be played by India. With its resources and strength it has responsibility for giving the lead to evolve and acceptable framework for co-operative relations[24]. The overwhelming edge that India enjoys in its size, population and economic and technological base makes it imperative that instead of showing up the inferiority or weakness of the smaller countries of the region. The continuing Indian pre-occupation with military strength to achieve a great power status is seen as an impediment to mutual confidence in the region.

Taken together with its ambitions for regional hegemony, India's dominant position in trade on account of it's huge market and developed industrial base makes the smaller countries of South Asia fearful of the consequences of removal of trade barriers in the interest of regional co-operation. While the landlocked members of SAARC, such as Nepal and Bhutan, remain heavily dependent on India, and amanable to its political pressure, the countries with access to sea have tried to avoid the degree of commercial linkage that could compromise their political dependence.

Progress in other core areas such as manufacturing, payments and development financing, is also hindered by fears of excessive dependence upon India, whose offers to facilitate increased exchanges by accepting adjustments in Indian Rupees enhance worries about possible Indian Domination. A breakthrough of sorts was achieved at the Islamabad Summit in 1988 when Prime Minister Rajiv Gandhi sought to allay the fears of smaller countries by stating that, "India has no hesitancy in declaring that it is fully conscious of its special responsibilities. We will not seek to secure any unfair advantage at the expense of any of our partners"[25].

The political situation in the Indian Sub-continent is

not stable. It is particularly so in India, Srilanka, Bangladesh and Pakistan. The last named two countries to divert the disenchantments of their people, propagate anti-Indian, rather anti-Hinduism sentiments. The Ayodhya incident of 6th December 1992, has given them opportunity of add fuel to the fire. Pakistan has gone a step further, New Delhi is convinced of Islamabad's involvement in adding terrorists in Kashmir, in communal clashes in different parts of India and traumatic violence in Bombay. Indian concern has been expressed in Indian Prime Minister, Mr. Narasimha Rao's tough talk during his discussion with his Pakistani counterpart Mr. Nawaz Sharif at Dhaka Summit. The President of India, Dr. Shankar Dayal Sharma chose the occasion of 89 the Conference of Inter-Parliamentary Union in New Delhi to underline the pressing need for identifying and eliminating the forces of state-backed terrorism. Many sovereign states have embraced terrorism as a highly productive instrument of state policy to promote their perceived interests. True Democracies, India is one of them, find themselves vulnerable to the terrorists menance the world over. It is high time that all countries stop viewing terrorism from the stand point of narrowly defined national interest[26].

There is no doubt that SAARC's future rests mainly with India. Its size and influence motivated its neighbours to form the Association as a way to contain the potential threat and to exert moral pressure on that country. They look to India to initiate regional 'confidence-building', to be more flexible in bilateral disputes, to open its markets for their products, and generally to play a positive but low key role in SAARC. The roles and attitudes of the seven member nations of SAARC vis-a-vis its evaluation as a strong Regional Organization do not bear enough evidence that they will generate sufficient economic forces in this decade or even in the next to propel SAARC automatically. All member nations must display a political will to forge ahead by taking into account the realities of the region and not allow a Declaration of any regional co-operation activities. Policy-makers, especially those in India, will consciously have to stimulate Regional Co-operation.

Their willingness to do so depends how they assess benefits and costs in terms of National objectives. While the task of strengthening and consolidating the SAARC process is mainly that of all the seven Nations, India has no doubt to preponderant role in this regard. The Association's contribution to Regional development would emerge as a by-product of a political process that will be successful only the countries believe that they derive political benefits from participating[27].

The SAARC has some other weakness too. To begin with it is still not fully representative Regional members like Burma and Afghanistan are not its members. While Burma has deliberately opted out, the cause of Afghanistan's membership has been vitiated by the considerations of regional and even global politics.

Besides the problem of representation, the very elaborate nature of the organization structure has created difficulties. These arise from the frequency of Summits and the associated meetings of other tiers. The levels of implementation and the availability of concrete gains in the agreed areas of activities in the SAARC have remained at a peripheral level limited to seminars, workshops, training programmes, exhibitions, etc. This is far from achieving people-oriented development as also National and Regional self-reliance, heard so often and so loudly at the SAARC gatherings.

It is true that notable ideas like the Food Security Reserve and Suppression of Terrorism have been given a concrete shape, but much of their implementation will depend on considerable bilateral goodwill and political understanding. The test of their utility would be seen only when provisions of these arrangements will be involved by the affected countries. Similarly there are bright prospects and immense possibilities of co-operation in the fields of cultural exchanges and movement of people in the region which, it seems, would be harnessed generally. On the whole, therefore, the SAARC progress so far has been slow and trady[28].

One of the main reason for the success of Organisations

like the EU, the ASEAN, NAFTA and the Gulf co-operation Council (GCC) is the convergence of political, security and ideological perceptions of their member Nations. But there is sharp divergence of views among South Asian States about political and security matters. A number of bilateral disputes have created on environment of mutual mistrust and suspicion among the South Asian political elites. Divergence in the State structures and political systems in South Asia has been an irritant and an obstacle in moving towards greater understanding and co-operation in the region. To some extent, a positive change is taking place in this regard. Mention may be made of the revival of democratic policies in Nepal, Bangladesh and Pakistan and Violence in the different parts of Pakistani Provinces Sindha and Baluchistan. In other South Asian countries to the forces of instability and turbulance have surfaced in the form of ethnic and religious extremism. Bhutan is experiencing its worst, ever ethnic crisis on the question of the states of its Nepali population in the Southern Zone. Srilanka is far from being relieved of its ethnic conflict and in India, serious questions have emerged on the viability of its secularism in the wake of the rise of Hindu fundamentalist forces and the serious insurgency in Kashmir which seeks legitimacy on the basis of religious identity. As a result of this political turmoil and crisis of governance in almost all the South Asian countries, the entire regional scene is characterised by instability and uncertainty and there are no immediate prospects of this situation improving[29].

The another fall-out of regional turmoil on SAARC are not positive. The spill-over of internal conflicts threatens the regimes instability and crisis of governance also prompts rulers in South Asia to receive bilateral acrimony in their search for political survival. A typical example in this respect was in the reaction to the demolition of the Babri Mosque in Ayodhya in India by the Hindu mentalists, the Bangladeshi and Pakistani regimes took up the cause, so to say, of Indian and sub-continental muslims in order to consolidate the Muslim fundamentalist constituencies at home. In doing so there was no realisation that in the long run, these constituencies will pose a challenge to the present rulers political interests. In retaliation, the Indian Prime Minister refused to attend the Dhaka SAARC Summit in 1993. This was, however, not for the first time that the SAARC bore the brunt of internal political fires. Srilanka's ethnic conflict prompted Colombo to vitiate the SAARC process many a time in the past.

The bilateral relationship which is most critical in the advancement of SAARC is that of India and Pakistan, Pakistani involvement in Kashmir and Punjab insurgencies in India and the competition for nuclear edge between them are the manifestations of this mutual dissonance between the two neighbours. For example, the testing of 'Prithvi' Messile by India and 'Gori' by Pakistan. The roots of this dissonance are deeply entrenched in each other's ideology, political dynamics and aspirations of power-status. With internal policies in each of the two countries passing through a phase of turbulence and uncertainty, prospects of mutual confidence and understanding cannot be seen as more than meagre, notwithstanding the efforts of dominant global powers such as the U.S. In this context, while Pakistan see strengthening of SAARC as a process of consolidating India's position in the region and consequently a blurring of its own ideology and status, India fears that a broader SAARC agenda that includes political issues might facilitate Pakistan's diplomatic adventures to frustrate India's role and legitimate aspirations in the region[30].

Alongwith the dark clouds on the political and security horizons, there are lurking suspicions in the minds of the ruling' elites of the small/medium peripheral States that the so-called "big-brothers" is waiting for an opportunity to pounce upon their hard-own freedom. Besides, it is often alleged that the South Asian States have the potentiality to interfere in the internal affairs of one another[31].

In the context of the degree of economic integration and political understanding achieved by the other Regional

Organizations, SAARC's record of achievements thus for is seen to be much less impressive. SAPTA is still rather imperfect and weak instrument. There is not much progress on taking finance, industry and energy on the SAARC agenda. The powerful orientation of each of the South Asian economies towards the West is eroding the political confidence in harnessing the region's economic potential. The adverse political relations do not help to liberalize trade barriers between or among the countries which are opting for trade co-operation to the fullest extent. A small State's trade expansion may be hampered if it is landlocked by a State which is superior to that in terms of size, economic and military strength. Thus, the geo-strategic vulnerability of a State can be used as a political leverage for economic exploitation.

The unequal size of market appears to be one of the most important obstacles to the expansion of trade in South Asia. The fear of possible Indian Economic Domination over the economies of smaller countries in a barrier to trade co-operation in South Asia. The strong industrial base, technological development and its comparatively restricted market have given India a predominant position in South Asia. The extra-regional export pattern of the SAARC countries is mutually competitive rather than complementary. Jute goods are exported by Bangladesh as well as India. Tea exports are shared by Srilanka, India and Bangladesh. Pakistan competes with India in the World's high-quality Rice Market as well as in Cotton Goods.

The achievement of complementarity in products under SAPTA may not be possible due to the absence of technical co-operation and development financing in the South Asian countries. All the countries are faces persistent trade deficits, and in order to reduce these deficits they impose stringent trade control measures through tariff, Para-tariff and non-tariff measures which apply with equal rigour to Imports from Intra-Regional and external sources.

The SAARC countries are extremely dependent on the Western countries for technology, capital and expertise. Lack of financial and monetary co-operation has limited intra - SAARC trade and circumscribed the region's access to adequate International liquidity. Lack of co-operation among Central Banks of the member countries of SAARC to stabilize the exchange rate is not found to be a favourable factor for mutual trade expansion as indicated by the experiences of existing integration schemes.

SAARC countries has lack of a Regional Transportation Network such as the Asian Highway Project and the Trans-Asian Railway Project, developed Inland Waterways with special provision for transit facilities for Landlocked Nepal and Bhutan, a Regional Shipping Lines with multimodal transport including Regional Ship-Building and Repairing facilities and developed Air Linkage by pooling together resources of different National Airlines[32].

However, bilateral distrust and hostility has continued to cast is long shadow over practically every worthwhile SAARC project or programme, for instance, there is not much progress in implementing the convention on Suppression of Terrorism and Narcotic Drugs and Psychotropic substances, as Pakistan continues to be a state-sponsor of Terrorism against India. Similarly, SAARC's demand for International Negotiation to eliminate the use and threat of use of Nuclear Weapons appear to be nothing more than the usual rhetoric, when five members of SAARC have voted for the legitimisation of Nuclear Weapon in perpetuity in the NPT extension conference[33].

A real reason for the slow progress of the SAARC in the areas of concrete co-operation perhaps lies in the disparate nature of the member countries economic systems and productive structures, on the one hand, and political dynamics and cleavages, on the other. Since the withdrawal of the Colonial Rules, the Independent (South Asian States have consciously pursued policies aimed at distancing their respective economies from each other. This was clearly visible in the case of India-Pakistan and India-Srilanka. Even Nepal and Bangladesh have sought to distance themselves economically from India in their search for political Independence and National assertion. Although, SAARC purposely eschews political and contentious issues, its survival is largely determined by the political environment of the region. Sharp religious and political cleavages provoke instability within countries as well as among them. Ethnic Sub-Nationalism creates domestic challenges that cross national boundaries. For example, the struggle of the Tamil minority in Srilanka has had a heavy impact in India, especially in the Southern state of Tamilnad. One member State, India is feared and distrusted by others, each of which has frictions with it[34].

The hope for the SAARC lies in the fact that positive developments in South Asia are possible and forthcoming. The positive turn in India-Srilanka relations following the conclusion of an Agreement between the two countries in July 1987 on the issue of Srilankan ethnic problem. This has not only brought about strategic convergence between the two countries, but also opend up the prospects of enhanced economic co-operation between them. A similar convergence has also come to be established between India and the Maldives following the former's decisive role in frustrating the coup attempt against the Gayoom Regime[35].

There are two implications of poltical situation for the evolution and growth of SAARC. On the one hand, the South Asian Countries will increasingly require each other's help in managing, if not resolving, the spill-over of internal turmoil, conflicts and ins,tability, by they related to political struggle or ethnic and religious extremism. The SAARC framework of dealing with terrorism and drug trafficking, though a useful mechanism, is by no means adequate to deal with the emerging and new challenges. Thus a greater and continuous state-level interaction and understanding is called for, which in turn will reinforce the political basis of wider Regional co-operation. It is therefore, time for such economies as India to reconsider their reservations on discussing, at least informally, regional political issues bilaterally as well as multilaterally.

No less important than domestic uncertainties and political turmoil in South Asia are bilateral relations for the progress of SAARC. India's bilateral interactions with Nepal and Srilanka have improved, resulting in greater political understanding and enhanced trade and economic co-operation. It is unfortunate that India's efforts to bring greater understanding with Bangladesh have not borne fruit even after the resolution of the Tinbigha controversy and India's strong desire to expand the substance and scope of multi-facted co-operation in the economic field[36].

Long term benefits have been achieved by SAPTA in many areas. Its potentials remain for exploration of natural resources, human capital formation, exploitation of dynamic gains from trade through maximizing various linkages and economies of scale, technological spurt and appropriate technological innovations. Productive efficiency originating from mana-gerial efficiencies on the basis of comparative advantage and augmenting efficiencies emanating from competition which act as catalyst elements in the development process of the region. Beyond these factors, the more SAPTA will be taking its institutional shape, the more will it strengthen the bargaining capacity of SAARC countries with the developed West. The emergence of SAPTA lies in the need for eradicating oblect poverty of the South Asian countries as well as the external fear of maginalization arising out of the ongoing global trend of Regional Economic co-operation. However, the South Asian countries have accepted the reality of trade co-operation through SAPTA with India at the heart of the region. The strengthening of SAPTA in South Asia depends upon India's gesture with regard to its concessions about the implementation of SAPTA[37].

Another very important factor which has been emphasised time and again by the South Asian leaders, is the urgent need to expand the infrastructural linkages. In our opinion, a considerable scope exists to improve the Road Networks within the region. It is a happy augurg that all the capital cities in South Asia have been recently linked by Air and Road. For example India-Pakistan and India-Bangladesh. The Shipping Navigation arrangement among these countries should be strengthened. Already the countries of the region are linked by Microwave. There is no reason why the entire South Asian region should not be, linked by a common Satellite so that there can be proper weather forecasting and an advance indication on the approaching Cyclone and Hurricans[38].

It may be no exaggeration to say that it is not possible to pursue co-operation in economic, social and cultural fields beyond a certain limit in the absence of political understanding and harmony in the region. Co-ordinated thinking and action on some of these problems at the regional level may produce better and quicker results. It such a trust and understanding is established greater harmony in strategic perspectives and security perceptions in South Asia will be facilitate. During the early period of SAARC, the deep-rooted political suspicion of smaller member countries about India had left them insecure. On the other hand, India thought that the smaller countries were ganging upon her. As a result, India and her neighbours have harboured an outlook of extreme caution towards one another. This kind of outlook has hampered the process of generating confidence essential for engaging in credible economic activities.

If political and strategic harmony is achieved, conflict and dissension will be considerably reduced in South Asia and many a new opportunities of co-operation will be opend up in the field of Defence. Mutual distrust and lack of understanding in political and economic fields in South Asia, therefore, are built into the prevailing structure of political economy of the region. Unless this structure is gradually modified and readjusted, it may come in the way of regional co-operation entering into a deeper and broader phase.

SAARC, however, has already proved to be a useful and unique agency for regional co-operation and it would seem to have the potential to function as a clarion voice of South Asia on the world stage. The SAARC members may not gain anything tangible, but the organization has its usefulness. Efforts should be made to make it work and serious thought should be given to making it a more effective body. This is a revolutionary era and Regional Alliances and Economic Organizations are being formed to make Economic Blocs for the mutual benefit of members of Regional Arrangements. SAARC is one such body that has the potential to assist the development of all members. There are other matters such as trade liberalization, economic integration, structured co-operation, management and exploitation of the Vast Water Resources of SAARC countries that need to be taken up seriously. All these peaceful plans for development can only be taken up when bulk of the irritants are removed and a significant number of conflicts settled amicably. SAARC without the fear of wars and without the fears of hegemonistic ambitions of any of its members can become an era where rapid economic development is possible[39].

Ideally SAARC should copy the European Union or such Organizations. There is no visa, no police check and not even duty restrictions. They are moving towards a single currency after having established a European Parliament. This is too far SAARC. But that is where the member-countries have to reach. Economically India will have to accept some extra-restrictions in SAARC. It is a good idea to develop the entire region with the help of member-states. The vast market of India should come in handy to all the countries. The problem is that of India and Pakistan. Both will have to be cajoled into orderly behaviour[40].

Regional Organizations are neither expected nor should attempt to find answer to all the developmental needs of the region. Particularly so, if there is no concerted effort by the concerned countries at the Bilateral and National level to resolve their problems. SAARC can only facilitate solution by creating a condition conductive to such a solution. And that role the SAARC has performed well within the given constraints. For example, India and Pakistan could agree to sign an agreement regarding not attacking each others Nuclear Facilities only due to informal consultations between President Zie and Prime Minister Rajiv Gandhi during the 1985 SAARC Summit in Dhaka At the Bangalore Summit, heightend Indo-Pak tensions on the question of India's major Military Exercise Operation Brass Tacks, was also diffused. In that Summit, even the Tamil Militants were brought to negotiation powers in the Tamil areas. Thus on the whole, one can say that SAARC gathering have contributed to a relatively relaxed region climate in South Asia[41].

SAARC is seen as a process that will generate goodwill and harmony in the South Asian Region and enable the member states to harness their full development potential for the common benefits of their peoples. It represents an expression of our collective will to forget the misgivings of the past and point to more increasingly towards a phase of active and beneficial co-operation. It provides a common platform for the members nations of South Asia to air their views regarding matters of International importance. For instance, the Environment Ministers of the SAARC countries formulated a common South Asian Strategy for the United Nations in the Conference on Environment and Development in 1992. South Asian countries, particularly India played a leading role in the Earth Summit at Rio de Jenario in Brazil and SAARC countries have also actively participated in parallel negotiations for conventions on climatic change and biodiversity. The environmental problems of the region have gained the highest level of attention among the SAARC member nations. In South Asia, the efforts have been made to make a modest beginning in forging cultural and economic linkages inspite of a clear divergence whether one like it or not, sooner or later, contentious political issues will figure in the formal discussions of the Summits. The revision of the SAARC charter to include bilateral and contentions issues, may not be feasible at the moment, for lack of consensus among the top leadership in the region.

The lines of action suggest themselves that they should

enter into contact and interaction with other Regional Organizations, notably those in the vicinity. Pakistan proposed co-operation between SAARC and ASEAN during the third SAARC Summit in 1987[42] Major industrial powers can invited to become regular 'observers' at SAARC Summits, as it the practice of ASEAN, whose Summits are regularly attended by representatives of the U.S., Japan, the European Community and Australia. In the case of SAARC, China should be invited in particular, for it is contiguous to four of the member countries and many major rivers of South Asia originate from its territory. The presence of China as an observer or even associate member would be reassuring to several SAARC countries. At present, the charter of SAARC does not permit to discuss bilateral and contentious issues in the regional forum. Even then its area is very broad. Except for bilateral and contentious issues, the SAARC can deliberate upon anything if all the members are so willing. The Regional political context is changing for the better and with the growth and consolidation of mutual trust and understanding, there may be nothing that needs to be avoided in the SAARC process. It may also be noted that the International Political Climate is also undergoing positive changes and South Asia's strategic relations with the Extra-Regional Great powers like US and China are considerably relaxed. The Soviet Union has collapsed now. So the other neighbours of India cannot take advantage of this issue, without the favourable support of India.

The point that needs to be grasped in the South Asian context is that there is a mutually reinforcing positive relationship between the bilateral and regional affairs. It has already been mentioned that the SAARC has helped create a positive bilateral environment in South Asia. It has also paved the way for easing of bilateral concerns and worries. Still it has to go a long way to become a model regional organisation. The perfect understanding among the member states can make it a shining game. For allround development of South Asia, upliftment of life standard of inhabitents herein, and to cope with fast changing International scenario, SAARC is a convincing device.

## References

1. See comments of Bhabani Sen Gupta on S.V. Kodikara, "Role of Extra-Regional Power and South Asian Security" in Sridar K. Katri (ed.), Regional Security in South Asia, cit. p. 61.

2. BLISS Journal, Vol. 9, No. 2, 1988, p. 253.

3. Dr. Maqbool Ahmed; Regional Studies, Vol. 10, n. 1; Winter, 1991-92, Quarterly Journal of the Institute of Regional Studies, Islamabad, p. 100.

4. Charter of the South Asian Association for Regional Co-operation, p. 3.

5. Dr. Maqbool Ahmed; Regional Studies, Vol. 10, no. 1; Winter, 1991-92, Quarterly Journal of the Institute of Regional Studies, Islamabad, p. 100.

6. BLISS Journal, Vol. 9, No. 2, 1988, p. 258.

7. Ibid.

8. Dr. Maqbool Ahmad; Regional Studies, Vol. 10, No. 1; Winter; 1991-92, Quarterly Journal of the Institute of Regional Studies, Islamabad; p. 101.

9. Jagdish Lal, 'Third Concept: An International Journal of Ideas', December 1993, p. 26.

10. SAARC; "The Urge for Co-operation in South Asia", Spotlight on Regional Affairs (Islamabad), Vol. 5, No. 2, February 1986, pp. 15-16.

11. Imtaz H. Bokhari, "South Asian Regional Co-operation: Progress, Problems, Potential and Prospects", Asian Survey, Vol. 25, No. 4, April 1985, p. 386.

12. Rasul B. Rais, op.cit., p. 71.

13. S.N. Raghavan, 'Regional Economic Co-operation among SAARC Countries', Sponsored by Economic and Scientific Research Institute, New Delhi and Friedrich Naumann Foundation, New Delhi, pp. 206-212.

14. Ibid.

15. Ibid.

16. Ibid.
17. Dr. Maqbool Ahmed Bhatty, "The Future of SAARC"; Regional Studies, Vol. 10, No. 1; Winter 1991-92, Quarterly Journal of the Institute of Regional Studies, Islamabad, pp. 109-113.
18. Ibid.
19. Regional Co-operation and Development in South Asia, Vol. 2, South Asian Publishing House, New Delhi, 1980, p. 224.
20. B.M. Bhatia, Food Security and the Agricultural Base in South Asia, CSCD, New Delhi, January 1983.
21. Annextures to the Report, Committee of the whole, no. 2.
22. S.D. Muni and Anuradha Muni, 'Regional Co-operation in South Asia, National Publishing House, New Delhi, pp. 44-65.
23. Dr. B.P. Rao, 'South Asian Regional Co-operation; A trade view'; (ed.) Satyamurty, K., 'South Asian Regional Co-operation', pp. 45-46.
24. Umer, Maj-Gen. (retd.) Ghulam, 'SAARC, Analytical Survey', Pakistan Institute of Industrial Accountancy, Karachi, 1988, pp. 122-123.
25. Dr. Maqbool Ahmad Bhatty, 'The future of SAARC', Regional Studies, Vol. 10, No. 1; Winter, 1991-92, Quarterly Journal of the Institute of Regional Studies, Islambad, pp. 104-107.
26. Third Concept, An International Journal of Ideas, April-May 1993, p. 5.
27. V. Kanesalingam, General Overview of SAARC Achievements; Marga, Quarterly Journal, Vol. 12, No. 1, 1991; Published by Marga Institute (Srilanka Centre for Development Studies); p. 16.
28. S.D. Muni, "Confidence - building Exercise", World Focus, Monthly discussion Journals, Vol. 10, Number 1,1989, pp. 4-6.
29. S.D. Muni, SAARC at the Crossroads; World Focus, Monthly Discussion Journal, Vol. 14, No. 7, July 1993, pp. 4-5.
30. Ibid.

31. Mishra, Pramod Kumar, 'Dhaka to New Delhi: One decade of SAARC', India Quarterly; 52 (1-2), June 96; pp. 85-86.
32. Sabbir Ahmed, "SAARC Preferential Trading Arrangement; A Preliminary Analysis"; BIISS Journal, Vol. 16, No. 2, 1995, pp. 165-196.
33. Rajesh Upadhyaya, "SAARC: After a Decade"; Mainstream, June 24, 1995; Vol. 33; pp. 7-8.
34. V. Kanesalingam, General Overview of SAARC Achievements; MARGA, Quarterly Journal, Vol. 12, No. 1, 1991, Published by MARGA INSTITUTE (Srilanka Centre for Development Studies), pp. 9-16.
35. S.D. Muni, "Confidence building exercise" World Focus; Monthly discussion Journal, Vol. 10, Number 1, 1989, pp. 4-6.
36. S.D. Muni; SAARC at the Crossroads; World Focus, Monthly Discussion Journal, Vol. 14, No. 7, July 1993, pp.4-5.
37. Sabbir Ahmed, "SAARC Preferential Trading Arrangement: A Preliminary Analysis", BIISS Journal, Vol. 16, No.2, 1995, pp. 165-196.
38. P.K. Mishra, 'South-South Co-operation and SAARC', Monthly Public Opinion Survey, 34 (10-11), July-August 1989, p. 15.
39. A.Z. Hilali, 'Regionalism in South Asia', A case study of SAARC'; Asian Studies, Vol. XII, July-December 1994, pp. 38-42.
40. Kuldip Nayar, "Musings: Male Summit, Gujral - Sharif talks and SAARC"; Mainstream, 35 (24); Volume XXXV, No. 23, May 24, 1997.
41. Jagdish Lal, Third Concept; An International Journal of Indias, December 1993, p. 26.
42. Ashraf Fahmida, South Asian Association for Regional Co-operation, Institute of Strategic Studies, Islamabad, 1988.

# Bibliography

Ayoob, Mohammed, Conflict and intervention in The Third World, Croom, Helm, London, 1980.

Agwani, M.S. and Others (ed.) South Asia: Stablity and Regional Co-operation, Chandigarh, CRRID, 1983.

Aggarwal, M.R., Regional Economic Co-operation in South Asia, New Delhi, S. Chand and Co. Ltd., 1979

Ahamed, Emajuddin, SAARC: Seeds of Harmony, Dhaka University Press, 1985.

Aiyar, S.P., Commonwealth in South Asia, New Delhi, Lalwani, 1969.

Alli, Tarik, Can Pakistan Survive? The Death of a Nation, London: Pelican, 1982.

Ayoob, Mohammed, India, Pakistan and Bangladesh: Search for a New Relationship, New Delhi, ICWA, 1975.

Bright, J.S. (ed.), Before and After Independence, Collection of Nehru's Speeches 1922-50, New Delhi, 1950.

Brecher, Michael, The New States of Asia: A Political Analysis, London, 1963.

Bhadur, Kalim (ed.), South Asia in Transition, Conflicts and Tensions, New Delhi, 1986.

Brands, William T., Moscow and South Asia, New Delhi, USIS, 1972.

Boyd, Gavin (Ed.) Comparative Regional Systems, New York, Pregamon, 1980.

Blunden, John (ed.) Regional Analysis and Development, London, Harper and Row, 1973.

Blackburn, Robin (ed.), Explosion in a Subcontinent: India, Pakistan, Bangladesh and Ceylon, Harmonds Worth: Penguin Books, 1975.

Bhyuiyan, Abydur Rahman, Economic Integration in South Asia: An Exploratory Study, Dhaka, 1979.

Baral, Lokraj, Regional and Extra-Regional Links and South Asian Co-coperation, Kathmandu, Centre For Economic Development and Administration (CEDA), Tribhuvan University, 1983.

Balassa, Bela, The Theory of Economic Integration, Homewood, Richard D Irwin, 1961.

Crane, Robert I., Regions and Regionalism in South Asian Studies: An Exploratory Study, Duke University, 1973.

Cloude, Hugh D., (ed.) Regional Development in Western Europe Chichester, John Wiley, 1973.

Chopra, Pran (ed.), Future of South Asia, Dhaka University Press, 1986.

Chakravarty, R.C. The Political Economy of India's Foreign Policy, Calcutta.

Carr, E.H. Nationalism and After, London, Mcmillan 1945.

Dutta, Dev (Ed.), Himalayan Subcontinent: Emerging Pattern, New Delhi: Rachna Prakashan, 1972.

Dharamdasani, M.D. (ed.) South Asian Regional Co-operation, Varanasi, Shalimar Publishing House, 1985.

Demko, George (ed.), Regional Development: Problems and Politics in Eastern and Western Europe, London, Croom Helm, 1984.

Ernest, B. Hass, The Obsolescence of Regional Integration Theory, Berkley, Institute of International Studies, 1950.

Feresh, Seymour, India and South Asia, New York: Macmillan, 1965.

Gupta, S. India and Regional Integration in Asia, New Delhi, Asia Publishing House, 1964.

Hussain, N.M.M.I. Prospects and Problems in Co-operation Among Small Nations in South Asia, Colombia, Marga Institute, 1980.

Iyer, Reghavan, South Asian Affairs, London, St. Anthony Papers, Chatto and Windus, 1960.

Jacob, Philip and James Toscano (Eds.) The Integration of Political Communities, Philodelphia, Lipincott, 1964.

Jackson, Robert, South Asian Crisis: India, Pakistan and Bangladesh, London, Chatto and Windus, 1975.

Jha, L.K., North South Debate, New Delhi, Chankya Publications, 1982.

Jones, Charles A., North-South Dialogue: A Brief History, London, Frances Printer, 1983.

Joseph, S. Nye, Peace in Parts, Integration and Conflict in Regional Oranizations Boston, Little Brown, 1971.

Khatri, Sridhar, K. (ed.) Regional Security in South Asia, CNAS, 1987.

Kennedy, D.E., Security of Southern Asia, London, Chatto and Windus, 1965.

Lozoya, J.P. and Bhattacharya, A.K. (ed.) Asia and the New International Economic Order, New York: Pergamon, 1981.

Levi, Wermer, Challenges of World Politics in South and South East Asia, New Jersey: Prentice Hall, 1968.

Lesfeber, Louis and Chaudhuri Mrinal Dutta, Regional Development Experience and Prospects in South and South East Asia, Paris: Mouton, 1971.

Leon, N. Linderberg, and Stuat, A. Sheingold, Regional Integration: Theory and Research, Harward University Press, 1971.

Lakdawala, D.T., Trends in Regional Co-Operation in Asia in Margaret Grant (ed.) National Development and the World Community, New York: Dodd, Mead, 1964.

Mahmood, M. Regional Integration in South Asia Perspective and Prospects, New Delhi, S. Chand and Company, 1987.

Maloney Clarence (ed.), South Asia: Seven Community Profile, New York: Holt, Rinehart and Wiston, 1974.

Mansingh, Surjit, India's Search for Power; Indira Gandhi's Foreign Policy 1966-82, New Delhi, Sage Publication.

Mishra, Pramod Kumar, South Asia in International Politics, Delhi University, 1984.

Moulaert, Frank and Salinas P.W. (ed.) Regional Analysis and the New International Division of Labour, Applications of Political Economy Approach, Boston: Eluwer Nifholf, 1983.

Murty K. Satya (ed.) South Asian Co-operation, Hyderabad: Institute of Asian Studies, 1984.

Myrdal, Gunar, Asian Drama: An Inquiry into the Poverty of Nations, New York, 1968.

Nehru, Jawaharlal, India's Foreign Policy; Selected Speeches: Sept. 1946-1961, New Delhi Publication Division, Ministry of Information and Broadcasting, Govt. of India, 1961.

Pandey, B.N., South and South East Asia, 1945-79, Problems and Policies, London; Macmillan, 1980.

Papanek, Gustava F., Pakistan's Development: Social Goals and Private Incentives, Harvard University Press, 1966.

Perty, R.K., South Asia, New Delhi; Oriental, 1976.

Prasad, Bimal (ed.), Regional Co-operation in South Asia, Problems and Prospects, New Delhi: Vikas Publishing House, 1989.

Qureshi, M.L., Survey of Economic Resources and Prospects of South Asia, Colombo; Marge Institute and Third World Foundation, 1981.

Rostow, W.W., The United States and the Regional Organization of Asia and the Pacific, 1965-1985, Austin Texas: University of Texas Press, 1986.

Rudoff, Lloyet (ed.) Regional Imperatives: The Administration Foreign Policy Towards South Asian States under President Johnson and Nixon, New Delhi, Concept Pub. 1980.

Robinson, E.A.G. and Kidros, Michael (ed.), Economic Development in South Asia, Proceedings of a Conference held by Integration Economic Association at Kandey, Ceylon, London: Macmillan, 1970.

Russet, Bruce M., International Regions and the International System: A Study in Politics Ecology, Chicago: Rand Mc Nally, 1967.

Satyamurthy, M., (ed.) South Asian Regional Co-operation, Hyderabad, 1982.

Sengupta Bhabani (ed.) Regional Co-operation and Development: Political Social, Technological and Resource Aspects, South Asia Publishers, New Delhi, 1986.

Sharma, P.K., India, Pakistan, China and the Contemporary World. Delhi: National Publication, 1972.

Singh, Lalit Prasad, The Politics of Economic Co-operation in Asia Colombia: University of Missouri Press, 1966.

Singh, Lalit Prasad, The Politics of Economic Co-operation in Asia Colombia: University Press, 1966.

Smith, Donald E., South Asia Politics and Religion New Jersey, 1966.

Subramaniam, K. (Ed.), Self-Reliance and National Resiliance New Delhi, 1975.

Tablet, Philips, South Asia in the World Today, Chicago University Press, 1951.

Umer, Ghulam, SAARC: Analytical Survey, Karachi: Pakistan Institute of International Affairs, 1988.

Uppal, J.S., Economic Development in South Asia, New Delhi, 1977.

Wadhva, Charan D., Regional Economic Co-operation in Asia, Ahmedabad; Allied Publishers, 1987.

Waqif, Arif, A., (ed)., South Asian Co-operation in Industry, Energy and Technology, New Delhi: Sage, 1987.

Weil, Gordon L. (ed.), A Handbook on the European Economic Community, New York: Frederick A. Praeger, 1965.

Yalem, Ronald J., Regionalism and World Order, Washington D.C. : Public Affairs Press, 1965.

## Articles/Papers

Abey Singhe, Ariya, ASEAN Experience of Regional Co-operation; Some Lessons for the SAARC; Economic Review, 17 (11-12); February-March, 1992.

Adiseshiah, Malcolm S., Economic Retionale of SAARC; South Asia Journal, 1(1); July-September, 1987.

Agarwal, Manmoha, World trading system and developing countries: Implications for the SAARC Region; South Asia Journal, 3(4): April-June 1990.

Ahmad, Sabir, SAPTA: A Preliminary Analysis; Regional Studies, 14 (2): Spring 1966.

Ahmed, Imtiaz, Post-Nationalist South Asia; Himal, 9(5): July 1996.

Akhtar, Payami, Bilateral Disputes Sour Relations; Third World International, Vol. 10, No. 9, September 1986.

Ansari, Iqbal A., SAARC Human Rights Commission; Radical Humanist, 54(6): Sept. 1990.

Armacost Michael H., South Asia and United States; An Evolving Partnership; Deptt. of States Bulletin, 87 (2124); July 1987.

Askari, M.H., Summit and Pakistan India Relations: Pakistan and Gulf Economist, Vol. V., No. 45, November 8-14, 1986.

Bahadur, Kalim, Pakistan and SAARC: World Focus, 14(7); July 1993.

Banerjee, Subrata, SAARC and Bangladesh: World Focus, 14(7); July 1993.

Bhatty, Maqbool Ahmad, Future of SAARC; Regional Studies, 10(1); Winter, 1991-92.

Bhatty, Maqbool Ahmad, Russian Perceptions on South Asia; Regional Studies, 12(2); Spring, 1994.

Bhargava, Kant Kishore, Delhi SAARC Summit: Malaise and Progress; Mainstream, 33 (31); 24 June 1995.

Bhallla, A. and Bhalla P. (ASEAN and SAARC); Ris Digest, 13 (2-4); December 1996.

Bhowmik, Debesh, Monetary Co-operation of SAARC: A Plan for a single currency; Southern Economist; 36(2); 15 May 1997.

Bose, T.C., United States and South Asia, the Nuclear Proliferation Dimension; Strategies Analysis 16(12); March 1994.

Chakraverty, Nikhil, Looking Beyond SAARC: World Focus: Annual Number 70 (11-12); November-December, 1990.

Chakravarty, Sukhomoy, Vision of South Asian Region: A Medium-term Perspective; South Asia Journal, 3(4); April-June 1990.

Cheema, Pervaiz Iqbal, Kashmir Dispute and the peace of South Asia; Regional Studies, 15(1); Winter, 1996-97.

Children on SAARC Agenda; Mainstream, 35(7); 25 January, 1997.

Dash, Kishore C., Political Economy of Regional Co-operation in South Asia; Pacific Affairs, 69(2); Summer, 1996.

Dastidar, Mollica, SAARC Decade Action Plan for the Girl Child (1991-2000); Mainstream, 31(17); 6 March 1993.

Deb Roy, Bibek, Intra-Regional trade in the SAARC region; Foreign Trade Review, 23(4); January-March 1989.

Dhanjal, Gurusharan Singh, SAARC: On the Move?; Mainstream, 30(12); 11 January 1992.

Ghosh, Bipattaral, SAARC: Some Major Immediments to its Success; Asian Studies, 13(1); January-June 1995.

Gupta, Anirudha, Issues in South Asia; Geo-politics or Geo-economics; International Studies, 34(1): January-March 1997.

Hilali, A.Z., Regionalism in South Asia; A case study of SAARC; Asian Studies, 12(2), July-December 1994.

Huque, Mahmudul, Nuclear Proliferation in South Asia and US Policy; International Studies, 34(1); January-March 1997.

Islam, Nurul, South Asia: Regional Perspectives and New World Interdependence; Developments, (1); 1992.

Khalid, Tamveer and Balooch (Akhter), Nuclear Shadow Over South Asia; South Asian Studies, 10(1); January 1993.

Kumar, Rajiv, Co-ordination of Economic Policies in South Asia; Prospects, Problems and Modalities; South Asia Journal, 1(3); January-March 1988.

Lloyd, Peter J., Regionalization and World Trade: OECD Economic Studies, No. 18; Spring (1992).

Magner, Christian, Regional Co-operation in South Asia; Review of the SAARC; Aussen Politik, 44(2); 1993.

Mehrotra, Lakhan, Dream Takes Shape: South Asian Association for Regional Co-operation: Review of International Affairs, 38(905): Dec. 20, 1987, 36-39.

Mehta, S.S., Industrial Co-operation in Regional Economic Groupings Among Developing Countries and Lessons for SAARC; Foreign Trade Review, 21(4); January-March, 1987.

Mishra, Pramod K., South-South Co-operation and SAARC: Strategic Analysis, 13(5): August 1989.

Mishra, P.K., Colombo Summit and SAARC: Foreign Affairs Reports, 41 (1-2), January-February, 1992.

Mishra, Pramod Kumar, Dhaka to New Delhi: One Decade of SAARC: India Quarterly, 52 (1-2), January-June, 1996.

Mohammad, Iqbal, SAARC: Problems and Prospects: Regional Studies, 11 (1): Winter, 1992-93.

Mohanty, Manoranjan, Borderless SAARC Region: A Distant Dream? Mainstream, 35 (26): 7 June, 1997.

Moshaver, Ziba, Prospects for the NPT in South Asia: Contemporary South Asia, 1(3), 1992.

Mujtab, Syed Ali, New Delhi SAARC Summit: Link, 37 (6): 18 September, 1994.

Nadeem, Abu, India, Kashmir and South Asia; Mainstream, 32(20); 2 April 1994.

Nayar, Kuldip, Musings: Male Summit, Gujral-Sharif talk and SAARC; Mainstream, 35(24); 24 May, 1997.

Patra, Saral, Bangladesh: Not Playing the Founder's Role; World Focus, 10(1), January 1989.

Prasad, N., The Colombo Plan: India Quaterly, April-June, 1952.

Prakash, Shri, China's trade with SAARC countries; Mainstream, 30(22); 21 March 1992.

SAARC Reports of the Technical Committee on Rural Development, 1984-87; South Asia Journal, 1(4); April-June, 1988.

Sabharwal, O.P., India and SAARC; World Focus, 14(3); July 1993.

Sen Gupta, Jayshree, Integrating South Asian Economics; Mainstream, 34(34); 27 July 1996.

## Weeklies/New Papers

Bangladesh Times (Dhaka), 8 Dec. 1985.

Bangladesh Observer (Dhaka), 11 April, 1993

Ceylon Daily News (Colombo), 18 November, 1986.

Dawm (Karachi), 11 December, 1985.

Deccan Cronicles (Hyderabad).

Daily Telegraph (London).

Economic Weekly (New Delhi), 14 October, 1961.

Economic Times, (New Delhi)

# Index